The Emergent Church

THE EMERGENT CHURCH

*The Future of Christianity
in a Postbourgeois World*

Johann Baptist Metz

Translated by Peter Mann

CROSSROAD · NEW YORK

1981
The Crossroad Publishing Company
18 East 41st Street, New York, NY 10017

Originally published as *Jenseits bürgerlicher Religion.*
Reden über die Zukunft des Christentums
© 1980 Chr. Kaiser Verlag, München
© 1980 Matthias-Grünewald-Verlag, Mainz

This translation copyright © 1981 by
The Crossroad Publishing Company

Printed in the United States of America

Library of Congress Cataloging in Publication Data

Metz, Johann Baptist, 1928–
  The emergent church.

  Translation of Jenseits bürgerlicher Religion.
  Bibliography: p.
  1. Christianity—20th century—Addresses, essays,
lectures. I. Title.
BR123.M5213   261.8   81-288
ISBN 0-8245-0036-9   AACR1

Contents

Preface

These talks, with one exception delivered during the last two years at Catholic and Evangelical Congresses and other ecclesial-social occasions, form an inner unity. The time sequence in which they are printed corresponds to a progressive unfolding of the one issue being considered here: namely, the beginnings of a Christianity that frees itself from the captivity of bourgeois religion and precisely thereby manifests its saving and inspiring power at the dawning of a postbourgeois age. In this age, the legitimate achievements of our bourgeois history of freedom will only be prevented from collapsing into a general barbarism if we ourselves at last cease to define our social and political identity—and also in a special way our Christian identity—without regard for the poverty, misery, and oppression of the poor peoples of this earth.

In this sense, I understand this book as a brief theological-political treatise on the future of Christianity and of Christian existence in a world which is determined by growing oppositions and, corresponding to this, by moral-political challenges which are becoming ever more acute and pressing. This challenge is above all a Christian one: we who are the Christians of the first world are no longer allowed to understand and live our Christian life separate from the provocation and the prophecy that thrust their way toward us out of the poor churches. Their cry for liberation and justice must be matched, in our situation, by the will to a conversion of hearts and a revision of life—a will which has certainly to take on an organized political form as well.

Statements about the future, especially those of a theological-political nature, are always in a special sense controversial. They preserve their will to objectivity not least by exposing themselves frankly to conflict and discussion. In this sense, I anticipate not only approval but also contradiction or even scepticism. This may already be provoked by the way the texts operate with too many symptoms and too few analyses—especially with reference to the critique of Christianity as bourgeois religion and the latter's function in society. In this case, of course, limits were already set to the analysis and to any comprehensive argumentation by the character of the texts as spoken addresses. I am therefore permitted to make reference in this context to my book *Faith in History and Society: Toward a Practical Fundamental Theology.* This book is concerned in a more comprehensive way with the problems of bourgeois religion and, in general, of a Christianity marked by the European-bourgeois Enlightenment and Revolution. It deals with those problems that are only touched on here in passing: for example, the question of the historical process in which Christianity and the bourgeoisie were bound together; the question of what has been called the dialectic of the bourgeois history of freedom, which in my view is often overlooked especially in progressive-liberal theologies, so that we then arrive at a tacit identification of the bourgeois subject with the Christian subject; the question, finally, of the bourgeois principle of individuation and the Christian principle of individuation.

My sincere gratitude belongs to both my collaborators, Werner Kroh and Christine Schaumberger, for assistance which went beyond the purely technical. For the dedication of this small volume to Karl Rahner, see the Epilogue, "On My Own Behalf."

Johann Baptist Metz

Translator's Preface

Throughout this book, Professor Metz uses the terms "bourgeois" (*bürgerlich*) and "bourgeois religion" (*bürgerliche Religion*) as the context for his vision of a new, emergent church. After much consideration, the term "bourgeois" has been retained in the translation since the usual alternatives, such as "middle class," "citizen," "liberal," etc., cannot communicate the many shades of meaning conveyed in this word.

The term "bourgeois" may originate in the European discussion, but the reality communicated by Metz in this word is by no means foreign to us in America. In and through this analysis of "bourgeois," he is inviting us to understand our own reality as the middle class, as white collar and blue collar workers, as members of the first world, living in a market economy shaped by the "bourgeois" values of competition and exchange, and so on.*

Equally close to us is Metz's use of "bourgeois religion." We are being invited to relate this to our own discussion and experience of middle-class religion, civil religion, industrial religion, the suburban captivity of the churches, and so much more, in order to see how Metz's analysis strikes deep into our contemporary problems. Indeed, the very way this book penetrates the situation of the West German church gives it a profound universality for an "Emergent Church" here in the United States and throughout the world.

Peter Mann

---

*For further treatment of this topic, see Johann Baptist Metz, ed., *Christianity and the Bourgeoisie* (=*Concilium* 125; Seabury, 1979).

ix

The Emergent Church

1.

Messianic or Bourgeois Religion?

To present critical diagnoses of so well organized and internationally respected a religious community as Catholic Christianity in West Germany is of its very nature a difficult undertaking. The problem becomes even more complicated when the attempt is made to locate the crisis in that very area where Christians in this country appear to find their identity: in the relatively large degree of harmony between the practice of religion and the experience of life within society.

The critical hypothesis which is to be verified in what follows begins with the question: Is Christianity in West Germany ultimately only a bourgeois religion—one with great value for society, but devoid of any messianic future?

Bourgeois Future—Messianic Future

When the church in West Gemany repeats the messianic sayings regarding the reign of God and the future disclosed therein, it is speaking primarily in this case to people who already possess a future. They bring their own future, as it were, into the church with them—the powerful and unshakeably optimistic to have it religiously endorsed and uplifted, the fearful to have it protected and confirmed by religion. In this way, the messianic future frequently becomes a ceremonial elevation and transfiguration of a bourgeois future already worked out elsewhere, and in the face of death the extension of this bourgeois future and the ego dominant within it into the transcendence of eternity. In the Christianity of our time, the messianic religion of the Bible has largely been changed into

1

bourgeois religion. This observation is not intended as a denunciation of the bourgeois, whose situation in society is not, as such, our theme here. Nor is it primarily a critique of the fact that the church in Central Europe is made up predominantly of so-called petty bourgeois and propertied bourgeois who, especially in this country, make church life what it is. It is much more the expression of an anxiety concerning Christianity, which creates a crisis of identity for itself when it fails to realize and manifest its difference from bourgeois religion.

In this bourgeois religion the messianic future is in the gravest danger. It is endangered not so much by its assuming an alien function of pacifying and consoling, becoming an opium for the have-nots who possess no future. The real danger is that of becoming an endorsement and reinforcement for those who already have, those with secure possessions, the people in this world who already have abundant prospects and a rich future.

The messianic future proper to Christian faith does not just confirm and reinforce our preconceived bourgeois future. It does not prolong it, add anything to it, elevate it, or transfigure it. It *disrupts* it. "The first shall be last, and the last shall be first." The meaning of love cuts across the meaning of having. "Those who possess their life will lose it, and those who despise it will win it." This form of disruption, which breaks in from above to shatter the self-complacency of our present time, has a more familiar biblical name: "conversion," change of heart, *metanoia*. The direction of this turning, the path it takes, is also marked out in advance for Christians. Its name is *discipleship*. We have to remember this if the future to which faith empowers us is not to be interpreted in advance under the spell of bourgeois religion—or, in other words, if we do not want simply to substitute for the messianic future our own future, the one in which we have long since been in control.

This Change of Heart Is Not Taking Place

The transformation of society is said not to be the concern of the gospel and not the task of the church; they must seek instead to change hearts. This is at once true and false. The conversion of hearts is indeed the threshold to the messianic future. It is the most radical and most challenging form of conversion and revolution, and it is so because transforming situations in society never changes all that really needs to be changed. But this means that this change of heart is in no way an invisible, or as it is often called, "purely inward" process. If we are to trust the gospel testimonies, it goes through people like a shock, reaching deep down into the direction their lives are taking, into their established system of needs, and so finally into the situations in society they have helped to create; it damages and disrupts one's own self-interests and aims at a fundamental revision of one's habitual way of life.

I want to express the fear (once again not in denunciation, but rather with uncertainty and sadness) that this change of heart is not taking place, at least not in the form it takes when publicly proclaimed. The crisis (or sickness) of life in the church is not just that the change of heart is not taking place or not taking place quickly enough, but that the absence of this change of heart is being further concealed under the appearance of a merely *believed-in faith*. Are we Christians in this country really changing our hearts, or do we just believe in a change of hearts and remain under the cloak of this belief in conversion basically unchanged? Are we living as disciples, or do we just believe in discipleship and, under the cloak of this belief in discipleship, continue in our old ways, the same unchanging ways? Do we show real love, or do we just believe in love and under the cloak of belief in love remain the same egoists and conformists we have always been? Do we share the sufferings of others, or do we just believe in this sharing, remaining under the cloak of a belief in "sympathy" as apathetic as ever?

It is no theological answer to this question to stress that, after all, conversion remains a grace. For theology has to take particular care not to let the appeal to God's grace be transformed into that graciousness we bestow upon ourselves, or confused with that indulgence we show toward the unchanging status quo of our own bourgeois dispositions. The same holds for the objection that such a criticism of contemporary Christianity ignores the sin in which Christians too are continually trapped, for clearly theological discourse on sin and the forgiveness of sin may not be separated arbitrarily from the messianic call to a change of heart. And when people insist that this change of heart is in the end a purely "inward process," this objection is not an article of faith but simply an ideology of our bourgeois religion, with which we conceal yet again from ourselves our own failure and refusal regarding conversion.

A *"bourgeois theology"* assists this concealment. In its theological discussion of the last things, to take one example, the messianic future has long since been relieved of all apocalyptic tensions: no dangers, no contradictions, and no downfalls remain. Everything finds its place under the primacy of reconciliation. But in following such a line, this bourgeois eschatology bestows, unknown to itself, a testimony of political and moral innocence on the present time, reinforcing bourgeois society as it is, instead of driving it beyond itself, according to the theme that everything will be all right in the end anyway, and all things will be reconciled.

In the same way, *hope* within bourgeois religion repeatedly conceals from itself its own messianic weakness, the fact, namely, that it is still awaiting something. Yet hope has to pay a very high price for becoming detached from expectations, expectations which of their very nature may be disappointed. Hope becomes a power without expectation, and hope without expectation is, in its essence, hope without joy. This, I think, is the root of the joylessness of so much of what passes for joy in bourgeois Christianity.

Love in bourgeois religion also seems to conceal from itself more and more its own messianic character. For messianic love takes sides; there was certainly a privileged group for Jesus, namely those who were otherwise underprivileged. The universality of this love does not consist in a refusal to take sides, but rather *in the way* it takes sides, that is, without hatred or hostility toward people, even to the foolishness of the cross. Does not the concept of universal Christian love lose all its dynamism and tension under the spell of bourgeois religion? Is this perhaps the reason it scarcely needs to prove itself any more as love of the enemy, since in the feeble and nonpartisan way in which it bridges over all agonizing contradictions it manages not to have any real enemies at all? Under the cloak of bourgeois religion, there is a widening split within the church between the messianic virtues of Christianity which are publicly proclaimed, prescribed, and believed in by the church (conversion and discipleship, love and acceptance of suffering) and the actual value-structures and goals of the bourgeois way of life (autonomy, property, stability, success). Underneath the priorities of the gospel, the priorities of bourgeois life are being practiced. Under the appearance of belief in conversion and belief in discipleship, the bourgeois subject—with an unquestioned status which even he himself finds inappropriate—is established with his own self-interests and his own future.

If I am correct, Kierkegaard's critique of "Christendom" may be understood already as an early form of criticism of bourgeois religion in Christianity. In fact, according to Kierkegaard, Christendom—without causing a sensation or even without noticing it itself—had more or less identified Christian existence with the "natural" existence of the bourgeois; a covert transformation of the Christian praxis of discipleship into the bourgeois way of life took place. In the form of Christendom Christianity had once again successfully come to terms with the power of the prevailing society, in this case with that of bourgeois society. Yet at what price? No less a price, so claims Kierkegaard, than the abolition of Christianity itself, the Christianity of discipleship, as he never ceases to insist. I regard this as a primary and eminently prophetic critique of Christianity as bourgeois religion, one in no way obsolete today, but— for both Catholics and Protestants—more urgent than ever before.

Rigorism Instead of Radicalism

The bishops sense the dangers which the practice of bourgeois religion contains for the life of the church. They are aware of the danger that the church will not so much change the hearts of the bourgeois as it will be changed by the bourgeois into the institution of "their" religion, becoming a church which is there simply to service their own security needs. Nevertheless, the pastoral approach of our church toward bourgeois religion tends rather to be one of resignation: it is a strategy of latent mistrust fed by the suspicion that in the end the bourgeois are not really to be trusted, and that they would ultimately overwhelm Christianity totally with their priorities and preferences if one were to give in to them in a single instance. So the bishops react with legal rigorism in those cases in which actual or supposed truisms of bourgeois society come into all too open conflict with the preaching of the church: for example, in the question of divorce, especially the readmission of divorced people to the sacraments, in family and sexual morality, and lastly, in the matter of compulsory celibacy. What I am saying here is in no way to attack the Christian ideal of monogamy, to make a plea for sexual license, or to oppose the eschatological-apocalyptic virtue of celibacy. The question is only whether such legal rigorism is the way both to overcome the contradictions of bourgeois religion in Christianity, and to make the Christian alternatives to a bourgeois way of life really visible. Or, to put it another way, whether this is the direction needed to heal the split between the messianic virtues of the gospel we preach and those which the bourgeois practice; that is, whether conversion leading to discipleship will become possible.

The rigorism with which the official church reacts to the crisis and sickness of church life indicated by bourgeois religion offers no real help for the grassroots communities at the parish level. They have to bear the full pressure of this contradiction. It is clear on this level that the rigorism of the church in its struggle against the abuses of bourgeois religion offers no salvation as long as the challenge of radical conversion is not clearly faced up to and risked as a community.

At the parish community level there is a particularly painful contradiction between the messianic virtues of Christianity that are preached and the bourgeois virtues that are actually being lived. The bourgeois virtues of stability, competitive struggle, and achievement obscure and overlay the merely believed-in messianic virtues of conversion, selfless and unconditional love for the "least of the brethren," and active compassion—virtues which cannot be practiced within relationships of exchange or barter; virtues for which one gets literally nothing in return, like the love which does not insist on recompense; virtues like loyalty, gratitude, friendliness, and grief. The presence of these virtues is diminishing; at most they are allocated, under the prevailing division of labor, to the family, which, however, is coming in its turn more and more under the anonymous pressure of the exchange processes permeating society.

In the family itself, the sphere to which the Christian virtues in their privatized form are allocated, the contradictions are becoming glaring. Here love is forced into a kind of diminished version of itself, becoming a love that renounces comprehensive justice. But where Christian love is lived nowhere else than in the family, it soon becomes impossible to live it there either. Like celibacy itself, the Christian family also tends to develop an isolated mode of life, which is exactly the tendency present in bourgeois society as a whole. The alternative to this, a way of life as discipleship, is not manifesting itself. The more difficult it becomes to conceal this contradiction of the gospel, the more emphatic become the church's appeals to family and celibacy as islands of Christian virtue—but also the greater becomes the threat posed to these, as I see it, by excessive legalist demands.

The *parish community* as "family" is threatened by the same fate which already seems to have overtaken the individual family: it is losing its young people; in other words, it is no longer able to integrate the young into itself with their criticisms, their alternative mentality, and their attempts at political emancipation. And yet there are still young people ready for the call to discipleship, there is a longing for a radical Christian existence, for alternatives to bourgeois religion. If these people are becoming increasingly hard to reach, if they have wandered off in the meantime to join other struggles, the fault is not theirs alone.

If this discussion of bourgeois religion is justified, this will be particularly manifest in the role which *money* plays within it. Money is, after all, a binding symbol of bourgeois society and of the principle of exchange which determines this society to its very foundations. An examination of the function of money in bourgeois religion involves more than the question of the quasi-ideological significance attached to obligatory church taxes. The central issue is the compensatory function which money in general has acquired. One aspect of this is its use by church authorities, where the removal of financial support, for example, is used as a disciplinary measure, and money becomes something like an aid to the achievement of ecclesiastical orthodoxy. But in addition to this, there is the salvational function of money for Christians themselves; money, often earned with a ruthless lack of compassion, becomes the substitute for compassion. Its function is to express solidarity and sympathy, to make up for that renunciation of comprehensive justice caused by society being totally permeated by the principle of exchange. Money thus becomes the powerful mediation between

the Christian virtues—which in bourgeois religion are restricted totally to the private sphere—and societal suffering; it becomes the
quasi-sacrament of solidarity and sympathy. To be sure, quasi-
sacramental as it is, money still manages to express something of
that reality which it cannot provide of itself; namely, the orientation and extension of our love and our compassion according to
those messianic standards for which there are practically no limits
to our responsibility.

The problem of the church's large-scale aid organizations is not
that they exist, but that in the minds of Christians in this country
they remove this necessary help from its all-embracing messianic
context (which includes factors like solidarity, political education,
and the will to practical change), and reduce it to a process of the
mere giving of money.

Radicalism Instead of Rigorism

My starting assumption is that the reason for the church's loss of
appeal is not that it demands too much from people, but that it
offers, in fact, too little challenge or else does not present its demands clearly enough as priorities of the gospel itself. If the
church were more "radical" in the gospel sense, it would probably
not need to be so "rigorous" in the legal sense. Rigorism springs
more from fear, radicalism from freedom, the freedom of Christ's
call. Where the church's preaching and pastoral work express the
priorities of the gospel, using, for example, the all-embracing strategy of love to attack the dominant principles of exchange and barter
as these spread insidiously into the psychic foundations of societal
life, and overcoming the reification of interpersonal relations and
their increasing interchangeability and transitoriness, the church is
then radical without necessarily having to be rigorous in the legal
sense. The church could then, to take just one example, admit to
the sacraments those whose marriages had failed and who were
seeking forgiveness for this, without having to fear that the floodgates would be opened. Nor would the church then need compulsory celibacy to mask a Christendom which had lost its radical
character. There would be no danger at all that the apocalyptic virtue of celibacy would die out; it would continually reemerge from
the radical challenge of discipleship.

Then, too, authority in our church would lose that bureaucratic face which everyone complains about; it would be able to take on more clearly the features of an authority deriving from religious leadership, displaying its administrative and juridical competence less and its religious competence more.

Politics–Morality–Religion: The World Context

How can we bring about a shift in priorities? How can we achieve a fundamental revision which will affect even the psychic foundations of bourgeois life? I myself can see only one way forward: we need a basic change of direction throughout the church, throughout society, and in world politics. This way forward would not be a detour, nor an escape into a purely speculative abstraction. What is really abstract today is that approach which "abstracts" from the worldwide interconnections in which our individual and societal life is entangled.

Our world, aware of itself for the first time as a whole, is at the same time riven with deep, agonizing oppositions which threaten more and more to become an apocalyptic gulf between rich and poor, the dominating and the dominated. Purely political and economic emergency strategies are no longer discernible or else, when tried, show their inadequacy. Only with difficulty do they cover over apparently irreconcilable interests. This makes many people bewildered and apathetic and drives others into hatred and fanaticism (the latter is a more likely result of the spreading apathy than any conversion to solidarity and love). Others again take up rigid defensive attitudes and end by adopting a strategy of self-assertion and internal security.

Everyone can see the signs of this looming social apocalypse: the atomic threat, the arms race madness, the destruction of the environment, terrorism, the global struggle of exploitation, or North-South conflict with its attendant danger of a worldwide social war. And yet the catastrophe remains mostly an awareness "in the mind," not in the heart. It generates depression but not grief, apathy but not resistance. People seem to be becoming more and more the voyeurs of their own downfall. Countermeasures are scarcely in sight—undoubtedly because the familiar strategies and prophecies are failing.

It is certainly not my intention here to mystify the "catastrophe," and by frivolously playing with this imagined total disaster bring into ridicule any nuanced approach and any new initiative. The contrary is true. My only aim is to make clear the necessary dimensions and the essential nature of the measures that are now needed. Must we not start with the assumption that the oppositions which are feeding this hatred and despair, or this apathy, can only be overcome without a catastrophe when a fundamental revision of existential priorities—in fact when a change of heart occurs in the rich countries of this earth, not just among the brutally rich grabbers among the oppressed nations themselves? Is this not the only way in which the poor and exploited can escape from their injured lives, stunted as these are from the outset, without erupting in an explosion of hatred? Are not moral actions now becoming a reality of world politics? Or, to put it the other way round, are not economics and politics becoming in a new way part of morality?

Christians are convinced that such a moral change of heart cannot be kept going unless it is supported by religion. They start from the assumption that when religion disappears, not only among the so-called enlightened sections of the population but even among the people as a whole, so that among them as well the rumor of God's existence is no longer believed, then the "soul" of humanity itself dies and in the end there is only the apotheosis of banality and hatred: the individual will become a machine, a new kind of animal, or the inevitable victim of totalitarian tyranny. It is precisely for these reasons, and within this critical situation we have described, that Christianity, with its moral reserves and its capacity for conversion, is called to stand the test of history. It is my view that nothing is more needed today than a moral and political imagination springing up from a messianic Christianity and capable of being more than just a copy of already accepted political and economic strategies.

The Church's Work of Reconciliation

The worldwide church provides us with a dramatic illustration clarifying this situation and the challenge it contains as it summons us to a change of heart. This is the relation of the rich churches to the poor churches, or, in general, of the churches of Central Europe to those of the Latin American subcontinent.

I am not situating this question of conversion within the perspective of the worldwide church simply in order to have an imaginary parade ground for displaying my aesthetic radicalism. This is no abstract speculation about the future, but a totally concrete question about the possibility of survival today for those others who are our eucharistic table companions in the one church—without even considering for the moment their future survival.

This new orientation toward the world church would also have yet another effect: I am convinced that there will only be a reconciliation between the traditionalist and the more liberal wings in our European church when the church's work of reconciliation makes its main task reconciliation between the poor and rich churches as a whole, and by so doing makes a contribution to the reconciliation of our agonizingly riven world. In other words, the program of sanctity must now be linked with that of militant love.

These poor churches are already manifesting to us this new model of Christian life—manifesting it in the witness of those countless Latin American Christians who have lived the messianic virtues of discipleship at the very cost of their lives. In these the productive model of holiness for our time shines out: holiness, not as a strictly private ideal one seeks for oneself and that could therefore easily lure one into an attitude of conformism toward the prevailing political situation but rather a holiness that proves itself in an alliance of mysticism and that militant love which draws upon itself the sufferings of others. Without any doubt, our age has its own martyrology. It contains the names of lay people, priests, and bishops who have risked all and given all in the struggle for a church in solidarity with the people. With them, these allies united by messianic trust, a change of heart becomes possible, the spell of bourgeois religion will be broken. Such a perspective shows how little the current priorities in the life of the churches in West Germany are simply, of themselves, "the" overriding church priorities; it shows how there can be quite different pastoral priorities than those that are central in this country.

There is taking place then in the churches of Latin America a process of conversion on an enormous scale, which in my view has a providential meaning for the whole church, and in which, in one way or another, we are all involved. In the last ten years (since Medellín), an upheaval has been going on there that could be described as a revolutionary changeover from a "paternalistic church looking after the people" to a "church of the people themselves." The suffering and oppressed people are thereby finally becoming the subject of their own history—not in opposition to the church nor by ignoring the church, but through the church and in the power of its messianic hope. This is why it could come about that one day in those countries, not just the oppressed people but the liberated people as well will exist as church. It is of course true that Christian hope exists also in a life that is oppressed. The messianic hope of Christians is, after all, much more a hope held by the slaves and the damaged people of this world than one held by victors. But the "successful" and prosperous Christians are the last people able to infer from this a strictly interiorized form of Christian hope to be imposed upon the poor churches.

Yet it is just this Central European bourgeois religion of inwardness which influential cardinals, bishops, and some working groups in West Germany seem to want as the new standard for the Medellín-church in Latin America—such a vision fills me with fear and makes me ask whether this is the price Latin America has to pay for the billions they receive in charitable contributions.

Sharing the fate of these churches challenges us to a fundamental conversion in this country. Only then can Christians here become people of help and solidarity. The direct struggle of the poor and oppressed people there must be matched here by a struggle and resistance against ourselves, against the ingrained ideals of always having more, of always having to increase our affluence. This is the struggle against the permeation of the whole of life by exchange and competition, which only permits solidarity and sympathy as an alliance of expediency between partners of equal strength, and which allows humanity to exist only when it serves someone's interests. A conversion of this kind, reaching down into the fundamental ideas on which our life is based, is demanded of us, not by some abstract progress of humanity but by the church as a eucharistic community and a sign of messianic hope.

Recently a Brazilian bishop (and it wasn't Dom Helder Camara!) wrote to me: "No German can say that he isn't an exploiter." A hard saying, but nonetheless spoken by a bishop. We Christians in this country have to live with the suspicion of being oppressors, although perhaps oppressed oppressors. This suspicion is not refuted by the fact that we willingly give alms. The demands of the love required here are not just satisfied by the "sacrament of money," for the very reason that the way this money was acquired itself increases the very poverty this same money is supposed to relieve. Clearly something more is demanded here, a radical process of conversion, a new relationship—one certainly hard to attain—toward social identity, property, and affluence in general.

Revisions

Where should this change of heart we have described begin to operate? Where can we initiate a transformation of priorities and change of perspectives? It can obviously only happen in lengthy processes of reorganization. I am totally convinced that there would be sufficient reserves of enthusiasm and of that power which flows from conversion in the church in this country also. Yet I venture to ask whether these energies are being properly called forth and "invested." For example, do the church associations, which are more or less all organized according to the social models of a past age, release the spiritual and social energies undoubtedly invested in them in a way that allows them to respond to the challenge we have described? Or, to put the question more critically the other way round: Why do the church authorities want societies only of this type, and why were the new-style youth organizations of the Sixties treated by the bishops with so much suspicion?

Or, to take up an earlier idea, could not the church's major aid organizations, which are more or less our only channel for showing solidarity with the poor churches, do much more than just collect money? Ought they not, precisely because they are aware that money is in no way innocent, play a powerful role in raising the consciousness not only of the recipient nations, but also, and especially, of the benefactors? In this respect, I believe that these important aid organizations, as expressions of a universal process of solidarity, are only in their initial stages.

There are signs that the Christians in West Germany are ready to learn and to change their attitudes. In recent years a suspicion, still perhaps unfocused, of the devastating effects of capitalism has developed at the grassroots level. Ecological responsibility is becoming an issue. There is a committed although relatively powerless concern about the plight of the poor churches and of the third world in general. At the Würzburg Synod there was a renewed attempt, at least in the form of a program for action, to take up the struggle for youth and, no less important, for the industrial workers. If our general pastoral approach in this country turns away from the defeatist attitude of a "floodgates strategy" and faces the demands of radical conversion, these new beginnings (scarcely heard of by the masses in the church!) in parish activity, youth work, or industrial mission would not have to be given up as lost before they have seriously begun.

When I mention here signs of a new messianic praxis, I am not referring simply to that process observable in my own country that could be called, or that some people want to label, a kind of "swing to religion," or "the return of society to religion." Recently, not only church circles, but also the political parties in this country are taking this phenomenon into account, but in my view it is profoundly ambiguous. The return to religion does not necessarily mean that a society wants to go, as it were, beyond itself; it may rather be invoking religion precisely in order to be able to remain as it is, to reinforce its own security needs because it senses in religion an accomplice in defending a threatened status quo. Where Christianity in this country gives way to such pressures of society, it may indeed become more presentable, but my fear is that it tends thereby to become even more that purely "bourgeois religion," which, in the face of the worldwide challenges we have mentioned, still manages to give our society a good conscience about continuing to live in the way it does. An authentic turning to religion on the other hand would have to mean: a turning to conversion, to the messianic praxis of love.

Discipleship as Class Treason

It is possible that what love demands of us here may look like treason—a betrayal of affluence, of the family, and of our customary way of life. But it is also possible that *this* is the very place where the discernment of spirits is needed in the churches of the rich and powerful countries of this earth.

Certainly, Christianity is never just there for the very brave. Yet it is not we who define the demands of love, nor is it we who fix the conditions under which it is tested. So, for example, Christian love in periods of nationalistic thinking may well have to incur the suspicion of harming national honor. In situations of racism it will incur the suspicion of race treason. And in periods when the social contradictions in the world cry out to heaven it will incur the suspicion of class treason for betraying the allegedly necessary interests of the propertied.

Did not Jesus himself incur the reproach of treason? Did not his love bring him to that state? Was he not crucified as a traitor to all the apparently worthwhile values? Must not Christians therefore expect, if they want to be faithful to Christ, to be regarded as traitors to bourgeois religion? True, his love, in which everything at the end was taken from him, even the whole majesty and dignity of a love which suffers in powerlessness, was still something other than the expression of a suffering with others, with the unfortunate and the oppressed, out of sheer solidarity. It was rather the expression of his obedience, an obedience that submitted to suffering because of God and God's powerlessness in our world. So must not Christian love in following after Christ continually strive toward that same obedience?

When the praxis of Christian love is placed under the sign of this obedience, which forbids us to confuse the mystery of God's will with the quite non-mysterious will to self-preservation endemic to our familiar patterns of life, then something of the messianic power of this love may be revealed. It strikes deep into our preconceived patterns and priorities of life. It has power to change hearts, power not to increase sufferings but to take them upon itself. It has the power to show unconditional solidarity, to be partisan, yet without the destructive hate which negates individual people. It combines within itself the program of holiness with that of militant love— even to the foolishness of the cross. Presumably such a "conversion of hearts" will in fact be dismissed by the experienced strategists of class struggle as feeble and useless, and branded as treason by those who are infatuated with our system of exchange and barter and whose rejection of the inhuman consequences of capitalism is at most only verbal.

What I have said may seem to many a considerable exaggeration. Yet what would a more cautious and "balanced" discussion of the messianic praxis of discipleship sound like? And how would caution and "balance" bring about a new perspective in the crisis we have been discussing?

For Further Reading

Bonhoeffer, Dietrich. *The Cost of Discipleship*. 2nd ed. Macmillan, 1967.

Fromm, Erich. *To Have or to Be?* Harper & Row, 1976.

Horkheimer, Max, and Theodor W. Adorno. *Dialectic of Enlightenment*. Continuum, 1975.

Metz, Johann Baptist. *Followers of Christ: Perspectives on the Religious Life*. Paulist, 1979.

––––––. "Political theology of the subject as a theological criticism of middle-class religion." In *Faith in History and Society*. Seabury, 1980, pp. 32–48.

––––––, ed. *Christianity and the Bourgeoisie* (=*Concilium* 125), Seabury, 1979.

––––––, and Jean-Pierre Jossua, eds. *Christianity and Socialism* (=*Concilium* 105). Seabury, 1977.

2.

Christians and Jews
after Auschwitz
Being a Meditation also on the End
of Bourgeois Religion

A Moral Awareness of Tradition

I am no expert in the field of Jewish-Christian ecumenism. And yet my readiness to voice an opinion on the question of Jewish-Christian relations after Auschwitz is motivated not least by the fact that I no longer really know—faced with the catastrophe of Auschwitz—what being an expert can possibly mean. So already that name has been uttered which cannot and should not be avoided when the relationship between Jews and Christians in this country—or in fact anywhere else—is being formulated and decided. It is a name which may not be avoided here, nor forgotten for an instant, precisely because it threatens already to become only a fact of history, as if it could be classified alongside other names in some preconceived and overarching history and thereby successfully delivered over to forgetfulness, or—amounting in the end to the same thing—to selective memorial celebrations: the name "Auschwitz," intended above all here as a symbol of the horror of that millionfold murder done to the Jewish people.

Auschwitz concerns us all. Indeed what makes Auschwitz unfathomable is not only the executioners and their assistants, not only the apotheosis of evil revealed in these, and not only the silence of God. Unfathomable, and sometimes even more disturbing, is the silence of men: the silence of all those who looked on or

17

looked away and thereby handed over this people in its peril of death to an unutterable loneliness. I say this not with contempt but with grief. Nor am I saying it in order to revive again the dubious notion of a collective guilt. I am making a plea here for what I would like to call a moral awareness of tradition. A moral awareness means that we can only mourn history and win from it standards for our own action when we neither deny the defeats present within it nor gloss over its catastrophes. Having an awareness of history and attempting to live out of this awareness means, above all, not evading history's disasters. It also means that there is at least *one* authority that we should never reject or despise—the authority of those who suffer. If this applied anywhere, it applies, in our Christian and German history, to Auschwitz. The fate of the Jews must be remembered as a moral reality precisely because it threatens already to become a mere matter of history.

Auschwitz as End Point and Turning Point?

The question whether there will be a reformation and a radical conversion in the relations between Christians and Jews will ultimately be decided, at least in Germany, by the attitude we Christians adopt toward Auschwitz and the value it really has for ourselves. Will we actually allow it to be the end point, the disruption which it really was, the catastrophe of our history, out of which we can find a way only through a radical change of direction achieved via new standards of action? Or will we see it only as a monstrous accident within this history but not affecting history's course?

Let me clarify the personal meaning I attach to Auschwitz as end point and turning point for us Christians by recalling a dialogue I shared in. At the end of 1967 there was a round-table discussion in Münster between the Czech philosopher Machovec, Karl Rahner, and myself. Toward the end of the discussion, Machovec recalled Adorno's saying: "After Auschwitz, there are no more poems"— a saying which is held everywhere today to be exaggerated and long since disproved—unjustly, to my mind, at least when applied to the Jews themselves. For were not Paul Celan, Thadeus Borowsky, and Nelly Sachs, among others—all born to make poetry as few others have been—destroyed by the sheer unutterability of that which took place at Auschwitz and the need for it somehow still to be uttered in language? In any case, Machovec cited Adorno's saying and asked me if there could be for us Christians, after Auschwitz, any more prayers. I finally gave the answer which I would still give today: We can pray *after* Auschwitz, because people prayed *in* Auschwitz.

If this is taken as a comprehensive answer, it may seem as exaggerated a saying as Adorno's. Yet I do not consider it an exaggeration. We Christians can never again go back behind Auschwitz: to go beyond Auschwitz, if we see clearly, is impossible for us of ourselves. It is possible only together with the victims of Auschwitz. This, in my eyes, is the root of Jewish-Christian ecumenism. The turning point in relations between Jews and Christians corresponds to the radical character of the end point which befell us in Auschwitz. Only when we confront this end point will we recognize what this "new" relationship between Jews and Christians is, or at least could become.

To confront Auschwitz is in no way to comprehend it. Anyone wishing to comprehend in this area will have comprehended nothing. As it gazes toward us incomprehensibly out of our most recent history, it eludes our every attempt at some kind of amicable reconciliation which would allow us to dismiss it from our consciousness. The only thing "objective" about Auschwitz are the victims, the mourners, and those who do penance. Faced with Auschwitz, there can be no abstention, no inability to relate. To attempt such a thing would be yet another case of secret complicity with the unfathomed horror. Yet how are we Christians to come to terms with Auschwitz? We will in any case forgo the temptation to interpret the suffering of the Jewish people from our standpoint, in terms of saving history. Under no circumstances is it *our* task to mystify this suffering! *We* encounter in this suffering first of all only the riddle of our own lack of feeling, the mystery of our own apathy, not, however, the traces of God.

Faced with Auschwitz, I consider as blasphemy every Christian theodicy (i.e., every attempt at a so-called "justification of God") and all language about "meaning" when these are initiated outside this catastrophe or on some level above it. Meaning, even divine meaning, can be invoked by us only to the extent that such meaning was not also abandoned in Auschwitz itself. But this means that we

Christians for our very own sakes are from now on assigned to the
victims of Auschwitz—assigned, in fact, in an alliance belonging
to the heart of *saving history,* provided the word "history" in this
Christian expression is to have a definite meaning and not just serve
as a screen for a triumphalist metaphysic of salvation which never
learns from catastrophes nor finds in them a cause for conversion,
since in its view such catastrophes of meaning do not in fact exist
at all.

This saving history alliance would have to mean, finally, the radical end of every persecution of Jews by Christians. If any persecution were to take place in the future, it could only be a persecution of both together, of Jews *and* Christians—*as it was in the
beginning.* It is well known that the early persecutions of Christians
were also persecutions of Jews. Because both groups refused to
recognize the Roman Emperor as God, thus calling in question
the foundations of Rome's political religion, they were together
branded as atheists and haters of the human race and were persecuted unto death.

The Jewish-Christian Dialogue in
Remembrance of Auschwitz

When these connections are seen, the question becomes obsolete
as to whether Christians in their relations to Jews are now finally
moving on from missionizing to dialogue. Dialogue itself seems, in
fact, a weak and inappropriate description of this connection. For,
after all, what does dialogue between Jews and Christians mean in
remembrance of Auschwitz? It seems to me important to ask this
question even though—or rather because—Christian-Jewish dialogue is booming at the present time and numerous organizations
and institutions exist to support it.

1. Jewish-Christian dialogue in remembrance of Auschwitz
means for us Christians first: It is not we who have the opening
word, nor do we begin the dialogue. *Victims* are not offered a dialogue. We can only come into a dialogue when the victims themselves begin to speak. And then it is our primary duty as Christians
to listen—*for once to begin really listening*—to what Jews are saying of themselves and about themselves. Am I mistaken in the

impression I have that we Christians are already beginning in this dialogue to talk far too much about ourselves and our ideas regarding the Jewish people and their religion? That we are once again hastening to make comparisons, comparisons separated from concrete situations and memories and persons, dogmatic comparisons which may indeed be better disposed and more conciliatory than before but which remain equally naïve because we are once more not listening closely? The end result is that the dialogue which never really achieved success is once more threatened with failure. And is not the reason for this that we are once again unable to see what is there, and prefer to speak about "Judaism" rather than to "the Jews"?

Have we really listened attentively during the last decades? Do we really know more today about the Jews and their religion? Have we become more attentive to the prophecy of their history of suffering? Or is the exploitation not beginning again, this time in a more sublime fashion because placed under the banner of friendliness toward the Jews? Is it not, for example, a kind of expoliation when we pick out fragments of texts from the Jewish tradition to serve as illustrations for our Christian preaching, or when we love to cite Hassidic stories without casting a single thought to the situation of suffering out of which they emerged and which is obviously an integral part of their truth?

2. No prepared patterns exist for this dialogue between Jews and Christians, patterns which could somehow be taken over from the familiar repertoire of inner-Christian ecumenism. Everything has to be measured by Auschwitz. This includes our Christian way of bringing into play *the question of truth*. Ecumenism, we often hear, can never succeed if it evades the question of truth: it must therefore continually derive from this its authentic direction. No one would deny this. But confronting the truth means first of all not avoiding the truth about Auschwitz, and ruthlessly unmasking the myths of self-exculpation and the mechanisms of trivialization which have been long since disseminated among Christians. This would be an ecumenical service to the one undivided truth! In general, Christians would be well advised, especially in dialogue with Jews, to show particular sensitivity in using the notion of truth.

Too often, in fact, has truth—or rather what Christians all too triumphantly and uncompassionately portrayed as truth—been used as a weapon, an instrument of torture and persecution against Jews. Not to forget this for a moment belongs also to the respect for truth in the dialogue between Christians and Jews!

Something else has to be kept in mind, too: When we engage in this Christian-Jewish dialogue, we Christians should be more cautious about the titles we give ourselves and the sweeping comparisons we make. Faced with Auschwitz, who would dare to call our Christianity the "true" religion of the suffering, of the persecuted, of the dispersed? The caution and discretion I am recommending here, the theological principle of economy do not imply any kind of defeatism regarding the question of truth. They are rather expressions of mistrust in relation to any ecumenism separated from concrete situations and devoid of memory, that so-called purely doctrinal ecumenism. After Auschwitz, every theological "profundity" which is unrelated to people and their concrete situations must cease to exist. Such a theology would be the very essence of superficiality. With Auschwitz, the epoch of theological systems which are separate from people and their concrete situations has come to its irrevocable end. It is for this very reason that I am hesitant about all systematic comparisons of respective doctrines, however well-intentioned and gentle in tone; hesitant also toward all attempts to establish "theological common ground." Everything about this is too precipitate for my liking. Besides, did this common ground not always exist? Why, then, was it unable to protect the Jews from the aggressive scorn of Christians? The problems must surely lie at a deeper level. We have to ask ourselves the question: Can our theology ever be the same again after Auschwitz?

3. There is yet another reason why the Jewish-Christian dialogue after Auschwitz eludes every stereotyped pattern of ecumenism. The Jewish partner in this sought-after new relationship would not only be the religious Jew, in the confessional sense of the term, but, in a universal sense, every Jew threatened by Auschwitz. Jean Améry expressed it thus, shortly before his death: "In the inferno [of Auschwitz] the differences now became more than ever tangible

and burned themselves into our skin like the tattooed numbers with which they branded us. All 'Arian' prisoners found themselves in the abyss *elevated* literally light-years *above* us, the Jews. . . . The Jew was the sacrificial animal. He had the chalice to drink—to its most bitter dregs. I drank of it. And this became my existence as Jew.''

Christianity and Theology after Auschwitz

The sought-after ecumenism between Christians and Jews does not, of course, depend only on the readiness of Christians to begin at last to listen and to let Jews express themselves as Jews, which means as the Jewish people with their own history. This ecumenism contains also a fundamental theological problem regarding Christianity's own readiness, and the extent of this readiness, to recognize the messianic tradition of Judaism in its unsurpassed autonomy; as it were, in its enduring messianic dignity, without Christianity betraying or playing down the christological mystery it proclaims. Once again, this question is not to be handled abstractly but in remembrance of Auschwitz. Does not Auschwitz compel Christianity and Christian theology toward a radical inquiry into their own condition, a self-interrogation without which no new ecumenical evaluation of the Jewish religion and of Jewish history will be possible for Christians? I would like briefly to develop certain elements of this self-interrogation which seem important to me; these contain, moreover, just as many indications of constantly recurring and therefore quasi-endemic dangers within Christianity and its theology.

1. In the course of history, has not Christianity interpreted itself, in abstract contrast to Judaism, far too much as a purely "affirmative" religion, so to speak, as a theological "religion of conquerors" with an excess of answers and a corresponding lack of agonized questions? Was not the question of Job so repressed or played down within christology that the image of the Son who suffers in relation to God and God's powerlessness in the world became all too adorned with the features of a conqueror? Does not the danger then arise of a christological reduction of the world's history of

suffering? I want to illustrate what this means by a brief quotation from the German synodal document, "Our Hope": "In the history of our church and of Christianity, have we not taken . . . Christ's suffering, in its hope-inducing power, and then separated it too much from the one history of suffering of humanity? In connecting the Christian idea of suffering exclusively with his cross and with ourselves as his disciples, have we not created gaps in our world, spaces filled with the unprotected sufferings of others? Has not our attitude as Christians to this suffering often been one of unbelievable insensitivity and indifference"—as though we believed this suffering fell in some kind of purely profane sector, as though we could understand ourselves as the great conquerors in relation to it, as though this suffering had no atoning power, and as though our lives were not part of the burden placed upon it? How else, after all, is that history of suffering to be understood which Christians have prepared for the Jewish people over the centuries, or at least not protected them against? Did not our attitude in all that time manifest those typical marks of apathy and insensitivity which betray the conqueror?

2. Has not Christianity, precisely in comparison with the Jewish religion, concealed time and again its own *messianic weakness?* Does there not break through within Christianity, again and again, a dangerous triumphalism connected with saving history, something the Jews above all have had to suffer from in a special way? But is this the unavoidable consequence of Christian faith in the salvation definitively achieved in Christ? Or is it not true that Christians themselves still have something to await and to fear—not just for themselves, but rather for the world and for history as a whole? Must not Christians too lift up their heads in expectancy of the messianic Day of the Lord? This early Christian doctrine about expecting the messianic Day of the Lord—what level of intelligibility does it really have for Christian theologians? What meaning does it have—not only as a theme within Christian theology (one mostly dealt with in a perplexed or embarrassed way), but rather as a principle of theological knowledge? If this meaning were operative, or if Christians had rediscovered it in the light of Auschwitz, it would at once make clear that messianic trust is not identical with the euphoria about meaning often prevalent among Christians, some-

thing which makes them so unreceptive toward apocalyptic threats and perils within our history and allows them to react to the sufferings of others with the apathy of conquerors. And this meaning of the messianic Day of the Lord would make Christian theology perhaps more conscious of the extent to which the apocalyptic-messianic wisdom of Judaism is obstructed and repressed within Christianity. If the danger of Jewish messianism resides for me in the way it continually suspends all reconciliation from entering our history, the inverse danger in a Christian understanding of messianism seems to me to be the way it encloses the reconciliation given to us by Christ too much within the present, being only too prepared to hand out to its own form of Christianity a testimony of moral and political innocence.

Wherever Christianity victoriously conceals its own messianic weakness, its sensorium for dangers and downfalls diminishes to an ever greater degree. Theology loses its own awareness for historical disruptions and catastrophes. Has not our Christian faith in the salvation achieved for us by Christ been covertly reified to a kind of optimism about meaning, an optimism which is no longer really capable of perceiving radical disruptions and catastrophes within meaning? Does there not exist something like a typically Christian incapacity for dismay in the face of disasters? And does this not apply with particular intensity to the average Christian (and theological) attitude toward Auschwitz?

3. Is there not manifest within the history of our Christianity a drastic deficit in regard to political resistance and a corresponding excess of political conformity? This brings us, in fact, to what I see as the central point in the self-interrogation of Christians and of theology in remembrance of Auschwitz. In the earliest history of Christianity, as was already mentioned, Jews and Christians were persecuted together. The persecution of Christians ended, as we know, fairly soon, that of the Jews continued and increased immeasurably through the centuries. There are certainly numerous reasons for this dissimilar historical development in regard to Christians and Jews, and not all of them are to be used in criticism of Christianity.

Yet in making this observation, a question regarding our Christianity and its theology forces its way into my consciousness, a question that has long disturbed me and must surely affect every theology after Auschwitz: Has Christianity not allowed too strict an interiorization and individualization of that messianic salvation preached by Jesus? And was it not precisely this extreme interiorization and individualization of the messianic idea of salvation which placed Christianity—from its Pauline beginnings onward—at a continual advantage over against Judaism in coming to an arrangement with the political situation of the time and in functioning more or less without contradiction as an intermediary and reconciling force in regard to prevailing political powers? Has Christianity, perhaps for this reason only, been "in a better position?" Has the two-thousand-year-old history of Christianity contained less suffering, persecution, and dispersion than the history of the Jews for the very reason that with Christianity one could more easily "build a state?"

In a sense, Bismark was on the right track when he said that with the Sermon on the Mount "no one can build a state." But has it then been an advantage, I mean a messianic advantage, that Christians have obviously always been more successful than Jews in knowing how to accommodate their understanding of salvation to the exigencies of political power by using this extreme individualization and interiorization? Should we not have expected to find in the history of Christianity many more conflicts with political power similar to the history of suffering and persecution of the Jewish people? Does not Christianity, in fact, manifest historically a shattering deficit in political resistance, and an extreme historical surplus of political accommodation and obedience? And finally, is it not the case that we Christians can recognize that concrete destiny which Jesus foretold for his disciples more clearly in the history of suffering undergone by the Jewish people than in the actual history of Christianity? As a Christian theologian, I do not wish to suppress this question, which disturbs me above all in the presence of Auschwitz.

This is the question that compelled me to project and work on a "political theology" with its program of deprivatization (directed more toward the synoptics than to Pauline traditions), to work against just these dangers of an extreme interiorization of Christian salvation and its attendant danger of Christianity's uncritical reconciliation with prevailing political powers. This theology argues that it is precisely the consistently nonpolitical interpretation of Christianity, and the nondialectical interiorizing and individualizing of its doctrines, that have continually led to Christianity taking on an uncritical, as it were, postfactum political form. But the Christianity of discipleship must never be politicized postfactum—through the copying or imitation of political patterns of action and power constellations already present elsewhere. Christianity is in its very being, as messianic praxis of discipleship, political. It is mystical and political at the same time, and it leads us into a responsibility, not only for what we do or fail to do but also for what we allow to happen to others in our presence, before our eyes.

4. Does not Christianity conceal too much the *practical core* of its message? Time and again we hear it said that Judaism is primarily oriented toward praxis and less concerned with doctrinal unity, whereas Christianity is said to be primarily a doctrine of faith, and this difference is held to create considerable difficulty for Jewish-Christian ecumenism. Yet Christianity itself is not in the first instance a doctrine to be preserved in maximum "purity," but a praxis to be lived more radically! This messianic praxis of discipleship, conversion, love, and suffering does not become a part of Christian faith postfactum, but is an authentic expression of this faith. Ultimately, it is of the very essence of the Christian faith to be believed in such a way that it is never just believed, but rather—in the messianic praxis of discipleship—enacted. There does, of course, exist a Christianity whose faith is only believed, a superstructure Christianity serving our own interests—such a Christianity is bourgeois religion. This kind of Christianity does not live discipleship but only believes in discipleship and, under the cover of merely believed-in discipleship, goes its own way. It does not practice compassion, but only believes in compassion and, under the screen of this merely believed-in compassion, cultivates that apathy which allowed us Christians to continue our untroubled believing and praying with our backs to Auschwitz—allowed us, in a phrase from Bonhoeffer, to go on singing Gregorian chant during the persecution of the Jews without at the same time feeling the need to cry out in their behalf.

It is here, in this degeneration of messianic religion to a purely bourgeois religion, that I see one of the central roots within contemporary Christianity for our failure in the Jewish question. Ultimately, it is the reason why we Christians, as a whole, have remained incapable of real mourning and true penance, the reason also why our churches have not resisted our society's massive repression of guilt in these postwar years.

Presumably, there are still other Christian and theological questions posed to us in remembrance of Auschwitz, questions which would open a way to an ecumenism between Christians and Jews. We would certainly have to uncover the individual roots of anti-Semitism within Christianity itself, in its doctrine and praxis. A continual and significant part of this is that relationship of "substitution within salvation history," through which Christians saw themselves displacing the Jews and which led to the Jews never being really accepted either as partners or as enemies—even enemies have a countenance! Rather, they were reified into an obsolete presupposition of saving history. However, this specific inner Christian research cannot be undertaken here; it would go far beyond the limits of this paper. I must also rule out here any investigation of the roots of anti-Semitism in those German philosophies of the nineteenth century which in their turn have lastingly marked the world of theological ideas and categories in our own century.

What Christian theologians can *do* for the murdered of Auschwitz and thereby for a true Christian-Jewish ecumenism is, in every case, this: Never again to do theology in such a way that its construction remains unaffected, or could remain unaffected, by Auschwitz. In this sense, I make available to my students an apparently very simple but, in fact, extremely demanding criterion for evaluating the theological scene: Ask yourselves if the theology you are learning is such that it could remain unchanged before and after Auschwitz. If this is the case, be on your guard!

Revisions

The question of reaching an ecumenism between Christians and Jews, in accepting which the Jews would not be compelled to deny their own identity, will be decided ultimately by the following factor: Will this ecumenical development succeed within the church and within society? Theological work for reconciliation remains nothing more than a surface phenomenon when it fails to take root in church and society, which means touching the soul of the people. Whether this ecumenism successfully takes root, and the manner of its success, depends once again on the way our churches, as official institutions and at the grass-roots level, relate to Auschwitz.

What is, in fact, happening in our churches? Do not the "Weeks of Christian-Jewish Fellowship" threaten gradually to become a farce? Are they not a witness to isolation far more than to fellowship? Which of us are really concerning ourselves about the newly emerging fears of persecution among the Jews in our country? The Catholic Church in West Germany in its synodal decree, "Our Hope," declared its readiness for a new relationship with the Jewish people and recognized its own special task and mission. Both the history behind the preparation of this section of the synod's text and its finally accepted form could show how tendencies to hush up and exonerate had a powerful impact. Nevertheless, if we would only take this document really seriously even in this final version! "In that time of national socialism, despite the exemplary witness of individual persons and groups, we still remained as a whole a church community which lived its life with our backs turned to the fate of this persecuted Jewish people; we let our gaze be fixed too much on the threat to our own institutions and remained silent in the face of the crimes perpetrated on the Jews and on Judaism."

Yet, in the meantime, has not a massive forgetfulness long since taken over? The dead of Auschwitz should have brought upon us a total transformation; nothing should have been allowed to remain as it was, neither among our people nor in our churches. Above all, not in the churches. They, at least, should necessarily have perceived the spiritual catastrophe signified by Auschwitz, one which left neither our people nor our churches undamaged. Yet, what has happened to us as Christians and as citizens in this land? Not just the fact that everything happened as if Auschwitz had been, after all, only an operational accident, however deplorable a one. Indications are already appearing that we are once more beginning to seek the causes for the Auschwitz horror not only among the murderers and persecutors, but also among the victims and persecuted themselves. How long, then, are we to wear these penitential garments? This is a question asked above all by those who have probably never had them on. Has anyone had the idea of asking the victims themselves how long we have to drag out our penance and whether something like a general "limitation of liability" does not apply here? The desire to limit liability in this area is to my mind less the expression of a will to forgiveness from Christian motives (and indeed *we* have here hardly anything to forgive!) than it is the attempt of our society and of our Christianity(!) to decree for itself—at last—acquittal and, poised over the abyss of horror, to get the whole thing—at last—"over with."

Faced with this situation, one thing is clear: The basis for a new relationship between Christians and Jews in remembrance of Auschwitz must not remain restricted to the creation of a diffuse sense of reconciliation nor to a Christian friendliness toward Jews which is as cheap as it is ineffective (and is itself, in fact, not seldom the sign of an unfinished hostility to Jews). What must be aimed at is a concrete and fundamental revision of our consciousness.

To take one example: This new dialogical relationship we are seeking, if it is truly to succeed, must not become a dialogue of theological experts and church specialists. This ecumenism must take root in the people as a whole, in the pedagogy of everyday life, in Sunday preaching, in church communities, families, schools, and other grassroots institutions. Everyone knows that new traditions are not established in advanced seminars nor in occasional solemn celebrations. They will only emerge if they touch the souls of men through a tenacious process of formation, when they become the very environment of the soul. But what is actually happening here in our churches and schools? Not least in our churches and schools in the rural areas which are held to be so "Christian"? Certainly anti-Semitism in rural areas has varied causes; yet not the least of these are related to religious education. In my own rural area, in a typically Catholic milieu, "the Jews" remained even after the war a faceless reality, a vague stereotype; representations for "the Jews" were taken mostly from Oberammergau.

Some historians hold the view that the German people in the Nazi era were not, in fact, essentially more anti-Semitic than several other European peoples. Personally, I doubt this, but if it were true, it would raise an even more monstrous possibility, something already put forward years ago by one of these historians: Might the Germans have drawn the ultimate consequences of anti-Semitism, namely the extermination of the Jews, only because they were *commanded to;* that is, out of sheer dependence on authority? Whatever the individual connection may have been, there is manifest here what has often enough been established as a "typically German danger." And this is the reason why the question being dealt with here demands the highest priority being given by both society and the churches to an energetic educational campaign supporting critical obedience and critical solidarity, and against the evasion of conflict and the practice of successful conformism, opportunism, and fellow-travelling.

In this context I want to quote, without pursuing her argument further, the thoughts of a young Jewish woman, who worked as a teacher in West Germany, regarding the Week of Fellowship: "There are two expressions I learned in the school without having the least idea of their significance. One of them is 'in its juridical form,' and the other is 'legal uncertainty.' Every event in the school, and I assume in all other institutions, has to be confirmed in its juridical form, even when this leads to senseless behavior. . . . Wherever I look, I see only exemplary democrats who, according to the letter and without any reason or emotion, observe laws and ordinances, instructions, directions, guiding lines and decrees. The few who protest against this and display some individualism and civil courage are systematically intimidated and cowed. . . . That is the reason why I do not fraternize with the Germans, why I reject the Week of Fellowship, and why my soul boils over at the empty babble about our dear Jewish brethren; the same people who today speak eloquently of tolerance would once again function as machines which had been presented with a new and different program!"

At the beginning, I mentioned that Auschwitz can only be remembered by us as a moral reality, never purely historically. This moral remembrance of the persecution of the Jews touches finally also on the relationship of people in this country to the *State* of Israel. Indeed, *we* have no choice in this matter (and I stand by this against my left wing friends). *We* must at all events be the last people to now accuse the Jews of an exaggerated need for security after they were brought in the most recent history of our country to the edge of total annihilation; and *we* must be the first to trust the protestations of the Jews that they are defending their state, not from reasons of Zionist imperialism but as a "house against death," as a last place of refuge of a people persecuted through the centuries.

Ecumenism in a Messianic Perspective

The ecumenism between Jews and Christians in remembrance of Auschwitz, which I have been discussing here, does not lead at all to the outskirts of inner Christian ecumenism, but rather to its center. It is my profound conviction that ultimately ecumenism among Christians will only make progress at all, and certainly will only come to a good conclusion, when it recovers the biblical-messianic dimensions of ecumenism in general. This means it must learn to know and recognize the forgotten and suppressed partner of its own beginnings, the Jewish people and their messianic religion. It is in this sense that I understand Karl Barth's warning in his 1966 "Ecumenical Testament": "We do not wish to forget that there is ultimately only one really central ecumenical question: This is our relationship to Judaism." As Christians, we will only come together among ourselves when we achieve together a new relationship to the Jewish people and to its religion; not avoiding Auschwitz, but as that particular form of Christianity which, after Auschwitz, is alone permitted to us and indeed demanded of us. For, I repeat: We Christians can never again go back behind Auschwitz. To go beyond Auschwitz is, if we see clearly, impossible for us of ourselves; it is possible only together with the victims of Auschwitz.

And so we could arrive one day, although I suggest this cautiously, at a kind of *coalition of messianic trust* between Jews and Christians in opposition to the apotheosis of banality and hatred present in our world. Indeed, the remembrance of Auschwitz should sharpen all our senses for present-day processes of extermination in countries in which on the surface "law and order" reigns, as it did once in Nazi Germany.

For Further Reading

Arendt, Hannah. *Eichmann in Jerusalem: A Report of the Banality of Evil*. Rev. ed. Penguin, 1977.

Fleischner, Eva, ed. *Auschwitz–Beginning of a New Era? Reflections on the Holocaust*. Ktav, 1977.

Glucksmann, Andre. *The Master Thinkers*. Harper & Row, 1980.

Haffner, Sebastian. *The Meaning of Hitler*. Macmillan, 1979.

Horkheimer, Max, and Theodor W. Adorno. "Elements of Anti-Semitism: Limits of Enlightenment." In *Dialectic of Enlightenment*. Continuum, 1975, pp. 168–208.

Küng, Hans, and Walter Kasper. *Christians and Jews* (=*Concilium* 98). Seabury 1976.

Kogon, Eugene. *The Theory and Practice of Hell*. Repr. Octagon, 1972.

Metz, Johannes B., and Jürgen Moltman. *Meditations on the Passion*. Paulist, 1979.

Mitscherlich, Alexander, and Margaret Mitscherlich. *The Inability to Mourn: Principles of Collective Behavior*. Grove, 1975.

Pratt, G., et al. *Peace, Justice and Reconciliation in the Arab-Israeli Conflict: A Christian Perspective*. Friend, 1979.

Rubenstein, Richard J. *After Auschwitz: Essays in Contemporary Judaism*. Bobbs-Merrill, n.d.

Reuther, Rosemary. *Faith and Fratricide: The Theological Roots of Anti-Semitism*. Seabury, 1974.

Sartre, Jean-Paul. *Anti-Semite and Jew*. Schocken, 1965.

Stendahl, Krister. *Paul Among Jews and Gentiles*. Fortress, 1976.

3.

Bread of Survival
The Lord's Supper of Christians as Anticipatory Sign of an Anthropological Revolution

The Crisis of Survival or the Social Apocalypse of a Dominating Way of Life

What does man live on? Whose bread does he eat? Which food nourishes his life? Nietzsche: "I am Zarathustra, the godless; I keep cooking for myself in my pot every kind of chance. And only when it is well cooked through, do I welcome it as my food. And verily, many a chance came to me domineeringly; yet still more domineeringly did my will speak to it—and at once it lay there imploringly on its knees." Bread of domination over chance, food of power and subjugation of the play of nature: Is this the bread upon which we live? Is that the food that nourishes us? But what then does Nietzsche's "Grace at meals" have to do with the pervasive question of survival today? Perhaps a lot, perhaps everything; it leads us, in my view, into the center of what is called our crisis of survival.

This crisis of survival, which is being discussed today as the ecological question, is, in fact, not least dependent on the problem of the overburdening and overexploitation of the nature surrounding us. For if we want to achieve new ways of relating to nature and to practice ecological wisdom, we cannot simply begin in pretended innocence with "nature" alone. Nature itself cannot become the principle of a new way of action without some kind of mediation,

34

without some permeation of nature through society and anthropology. Otherwise we would be driven only too easily, as our most recent German history leads us to fear, into typically fascistic attitudes (of "blood and soil"). We have to begin with the history human beings have with nature. But this is a history of domination, a history of subjugation.

At the beginning of what we call "the Modern Age," the limits of which we are now reaching with ever-increasing clarity, there unfolds—embryonically and overlaid with many religious and cultural symbols—this anthropology of domination. In it man understands himself as a dominating, subjugating individual over against nature; his knowledge becomes, above all, knowledge via domination, and his praxis is one of exerting power over nature. In this dominating subjugation, in this activity of exploitation and reification, in this seizing power over nature, man's identity is formed. Man *is* by subjugating. All non-dominating human virtues such as gratitude and friendliness, the capacity for suffering and sympathy, grief and tenderness, recede into the background. They are deprived of social and cultural power or, at best, in a treacherous "division of labor" they are entrusted to women, who are deprived of power anyway in this dominating male culture. These nondominating attitudes become undervalued also as unique kinds of knowledge. What dominates is knowledge as subjugation: knowing as "grasping," as "appropriating," as a kind of taking possession. Other forms of sensitive-intuitive access to reality, such as through the eyes and their gaze, are forced aside into the realm of the private and the irrational.

In the meantime, this principle of subjugation has long since permeated the psychic foundations of our total sociocultural life. It has become the secret regulating principle of all interpersonal relationships; the psychosocial pathologies of our times provide a surfeit of illustrative material on this. In this sense, we could and should speak, not only—and not even primarily—of a poisoning through unrestricted technical exploitation of the outer nature surrounding man, but also of a poisoning of the inner nature of man himself. An identity thus formed through the principles of domination and subjugation makes the individual profoundly disconnected and, in the strict sense of the term, egoistic. It makes the human being incapable of seeing himself and judging himself through the eyes of his victims.

These marks of a dominating anthropology may have long since escaped us, since the drive to subjugation which belongs to this form of anthropological identity shifted its focus very early on outwards—against foreign minorities, foreign races, and foreign cultures. The European history of colonization has its roots therein, and the fact that the history of Christian missions accompanied this all too closely, arching, as it were, over this history of subjugation, may serve as an illustration of the pervasive way the mechanism of subjugation has also penetrated our church life and religious life. In a kind of objective cynicism, we speak frequently today of so-called underdeveloped peoples. When we look more closely, it is often a question of peoples whose cultures we have subjugated, devastated, and exploited.

This anthropological model of man as an essentially dominating kind of being is intrinsic to our European scientific-technological civilization. The inner tendency of natural science and large-scale technology will not be anthropologically neutralized by the fact that technology in both the major social systems, in Western bourgeois capitalism as well as in the hitherto existing forms of socialism, is employed as a supposedly neutral instrument. On the contrary, it is precisely this societal concealment which makes possible the most tenacious and all-pervasive efficacy of the anthropological principle of subjugation intrinsic to it. It is hard to doubt, for example, that bourgeois identity is formed in its very essence by such a principle. And where would the struggle for what could be called a new, postbourgeois human being be so successful that we would not discover again in this human being those same features of domination, and could, therefore, gaze on his image without fear?

This necessarily brief analysis is not, however, accompanied by the expectation of a gradual euthanasia of natural science and large-scale technology in general. It is rather a question of using these more critically and with greater caution; above all, of not exposing ourselves (or at least much less than before) to the anonymous pressure of the anthropology of domination intrinsic to them. The basic issue is that we should not let the concept of "life" be secretly presented and defined for us from that direction. And the anthropological revolution this entails goes to the very roots; its dimensions are given by the way in which the model of domination has long since permeated everything; this revolution affects the whole societal construction of our reality, of our political and economic systems. This fact is causing the massive helplessness and fear we see today; apathy or resignation are already eating away at the soul. Overnight, our dominating dreams of progress have collapsed into contagious fears for survival.

Yet the paradox is this: When life aims only at survival, even that success will soon be denied it. We will, in fact, only survive, only save our lives, when we understand what life is about. And so I repeat the question we began with: "What does man live on? Whose bread does he eat? Which food nourishes his life?" What is this deprivation which is depriving us of life itself, making it in any case weaker, almost invisible?

Living on the "Bread of Life"

At the center of their eucharistic community, Christians recall the passion, death, and resurrection of him who—in the language of John's Gospel—said of himself: "I am the bread of life" (6:35, 48). And in the same gospel, we hear also that word concerning the food from which this life is once more secretly nourished: "My food is to do the will of him who sent me" (4:34). Nietzsche formulated it very differently.

Living on this "bread of life" is not without its danger, once we have grown all too used to that other nourishment provided for us by the anthropology of domination, of the will to power and to subjugation. A serious changeover to this "bread of life" can make us at first downright sick, at least in the eyes of those obsessed with normality. But this will be a "sickness unto life"—to that life without which life itself perhaps will soon no longer survive. This bread can become for us the nourishment and sacrament of life, precisely because in the midst of our life of domination it gives visible shape to death, suffering, love, fear, and grief, and gives us power to take these into ourselves. Of course, only a few aspects of all this can be developed here.

1. This eucharistic "bread of life" makes us receptive to death. It draws death, as it were, back into life, allows death a renewed place in our life, so that this life might indeed become something

other than pure survival. It is, in fact, not death itself which alien-ates us from ourselves and snatches life from us: it is, instead, the suppression of death, the flight from death. This suppression of death has made us into those dominating beings bent on subjugation who today are everywhere encountering the limits of their survival.

For what is the real background to this process of subjugation, exploitation, and reification of nature that marks our history of progress? Does not man experience in this nature—a nature that confronts him as something alien and indifferent, and whose waves will roll over him tomorrow as they do the grains of sand at the ocean—his own death and his own downfall? And is not, therefore, the aggressive, unrestrained, total subjuation of this nature ulti-mately the attempt made by man as dominator to remove death from the world? In this sense, is not our scientific-technological civilization with its drive toward the total subjugation of nature a single gigantomachy of the repression of death? Is not the infinite path of our progress, in essence, a way of escape, a way to flee death? And whither does it lead us? Into life? The repression of death has made us into insatiable subjugators. Yet, in the mean-time, have we not long since become subjected to our own princi-ple of subjugation, that principle of domination in which all life rich in relationships is being increasingly extinguished? Subjected to that power of domination which can only repress death by pro-ducing in its turn ever new dead relationships, so that the question of a life before death is becoming increasingly reduced to the ques-tion of naked survival?

2. The eucharistic ''bread of life'' strengthens us in our receptiv-ity toward suffering and those who suffer. A life nourished by this bread allows suffering to exist in a new way, makes the sufferings of others visible, so as to transform them into our own. Here again it is not suffering as such which alienates us from ourselves and robs us of life—it is rather the repression and reification of suffer-ing, the pure flight from suffering. Only when people themselves remain capable of suffering, do they refrain from forcing suffering arbitrarily upon others, and are able and ready in their own way to share in the sufferings of others and become active in the liberation struggles of the tortured and the exploited. The same Nietzsche

who forces into submission all sufferings afflicting him and cooks them into the food of his domineering will becomes the great enemy of compassion toward the sufferings of others. The culture of the subjugators is one of apathy and disconnectedness from others. Their support is given to the suffering only when this enables them to come to power once more and thereby confirm their unbroken domination.

A eucharistic community nourished by the "bread of life" draws the capacity for suffering back into the life of apathy. It attempts to give this ability to suffer a new power to exist and to endure within a rapacious society which, in its revealing way, often simply covers up its suffering cosmetically, deadens it with painkillers, or seeks to organize it away through paternalistic bureaucracies designed to make suffering socially invisible. The question, of course, is: Do we Christians really let ourselves be nourished by the "bread of life" in a life-giving direction, toward the capacity for suffering? Or do we simply believe in compassion and remain under the cloak of a mere belief in compassion fixed within the apathy which accompanies life as domination? Does the sacrament of this bread really make the invisible sufferings of the brethren visible to us, so that through sharing in their suffering we may pass over from death into life? Does it give us back that power which we have lost under the domination of the principle of subjugation, that power which lets us look at ourselves and judge ourselves with the eyes of our own victims?

What kind of receptivity, for example, do we have toward the fact that our Christianity is itself generating profound and anguishing social oppositions, which are also class oppositions between the rich and poor churches. Through such oppositions Christians, as long as they remain in their apathy, are literally bringing death each day to those other Christians who are their table companions at the eucharistic meal? In this context, what has been called "The Text on Hope" of the Catholic synod in West Germany, puts it this way:

> In our service to the one church, we cannot allow it to happen that church life in the Western world should more and more give the impression of a religion of prosperity and satiety, whereas in other parts of the world it looks like a common religion of the unfortunate, whose lack of bread literally excludes them from our eucharistic table

fellowship. Otherwise, there emerges before the gaze of the world the
scandal of a church combining within itself the unfortunate and the
spectators of misfortune, the many sufferers and the many Pilates, and
calling this whole reality the one table fellowship of believers, the one
People of God.

Are we this scandal or are we not? Is our Eucharist a cult of life or
of apathy?

3. The eucharistic "bread of life" nourishes us toward love. It
wants to bring love back into the life of domination, and exorcize
that interiorized capitalism, that attitude of grasping and struggling
for advantage. "Those who possess their life will lose it, and those
who hold it worthless will gain it." We have every reason, confronted by this shocking saying, to feel fear—at least if we had
decided just to believe in love, but under the cloak of mere belief
to remain the same dominating egoists, men of subjugation and
power who have long since subjected everything they call "love"
to this principle of domination and who now practice this "love"
as subordinational and paternalistic love within marriage, family,
and society. Yet to repeat again: It is not, in fact, the kind of love
that forgets its own advantage and possessions which alienates us
from ourselves and robs us of life, but rather the very repression of
this love, the flight from love, and that prohibition of love secretly
dominating our modern societies.

Where Christians truly nourish themselves from the food of this
love, their eucharistic community will become the symbol and the
provocation for a new and unprecedented praxis of sharing among
themselves and with others. And much toward which this love
drives us may appear as a form of betrayal, a betrayal of our existing prosperity and property, a betrayal of our bourgeois class and
of the ingrained ideals of our life of domination.

4. The "bread of life" becomes for us finally the food of
mourning and of fear. The life to which this bread nourishes us
does not want to make us invulnerable and unassailable. The eucharistic prayers refuse, therefore, to become for us an imaginary
ladder allowing us to climb swiftly away beyond our own fears and
our own grief. Accordingly, the eucharistic bread wants to give us

strength, not for the hasty suppression of fear and mourning, nor for a swift recovery from these, but rather in order to let them exist. And once again: It is not the mourning and fear which alienate us from ourselves and rob us of life, but rather the repression of fear and grief, the flight from mourning. That famous saying about the "inability to mourn" is not just a statement within social pathology about the German mentality in the postwar years; it is a fundamental statement about every form of humanity which builds up its own identity through subjugation and domination. This subjugating form of humanity stands under a downright prohibition of mourning and melancholy; it is accompanied by the denunciation of grief as an unbecoming, helpless sentimentality. These prohibitions of mourning and melancholy in East and West—nowhere decreed but everywhere effective—speak indeed a language of their own. And this kind of humanity stands under the prohibition of fear; for its ruling principle of domination and power defines freedom in complete opposition to experiences such as grief and fear, which possess value neither for domination nor for exchange. This suppressed fear, however, throws people back again upon the supposedly unassailable life of domination and robs them in the end of all phantasy regarding their search for life, and what deserves the name of life.

What does man live on? Whose bread does he eat? Which food nourishes his life? Why has he lost hold of life so that he is fearful about his very survival? I make bold to say: The eucharistic "bread of life" provokes those who are nourished by it, and who make it their life's food, to begin a kind of "anthropological revolution." This would be what we could call the specifically Christian way of dealing with the crisis of survival prevailing today, a crisis which is not primarily a cosmological problem but an anthropological and political one. I cannot see how, without such a revolution, a way out of this crisis of survival that does not involve some kind of catastrophe is possible at all. If we Christians do not want to become mere helpers in the survival strategy of the already rich and powerful peoples, a strategy that will in every way increase the burden of the poor and long exploited human beings, we have to risk this anthropological revolution and prepare a rebellion against the catastrophe "which consists in the fact that everything keeps going on as before" (W. Benjamin).

Anthropological Revolution

That anthropological revolution which is now to be described in an extremely abbreviated form is without analogy in the modern history of revolution. Perhaps we could describe it as a revolutionary formation process for a new subjectivity. Yet such an expression is open to misunderstanding. In any case, it is a process of liberation we are discussing. And the theology aiming at this process of liberation would be that "theology of liberation" to which we are challenged and which is required of us in our situation, so that we might not betray or leave in the lurch—or even denounce as downright un-Christian—that other theology of liberation in the countries on the shadow side of this earth.

The process of liberation generated by the anthropological revolution differs, both in its inner content and in its outer direction, from the ideas of social revolution current among us. For this revolution is not, in fact, concerned with liberating us from our poverty and misery, but rather from our wealth and our totally excessive prosperity. It is not a liberation from what we lack, but from our consumerism in which we are ultimately consuming our very selves. It is not a liberation from our state of oppression, but from the untransformed praxis of our own wishes and desires. It is not a liberation from our powerlessness, but from our own form of predominance. It frees us, not from the state of being dominated but from that of dominating; not from our sufferings but from our apathy; not from our guilt but from our innocence, or rather from that delusion of innocence which the life of domination has long since spread out through our souls. This revolution seeks to bring to power precisely the nondominating virtues and, in fact, in this context to liberate our society also from a culture dominated totally by males. It is not surprising that for this kind of revolution no basis exists among the masses, everything remains extremely nebulous. The bearers of this revolution are scarcely identifiable and its formulation in political terms remains vague. I will deal with these issues a little later on.

First, however, the contradiction has to be explained between the anthropological revolution and our prevailing ideas about what revolutions are. Marx once described them as the locomotive of world history. Walter Benjamin has made the following critically reflective commentary on that statement: "Perhaps the opposite is really the case. Perhaps revolutions happen when the human race, riding within this train, pulls the emergency brake." This would be revolution, not as a dramatically accelerated progress, nor as aggressively heightened evolution, but rather as a rebellion against the fact that "everything keeps going on as before." This would be revolution as interruption, which seems to me exactly the direction aimed at by the anthropological revolution. We Christians possess a central word for this: conversion, the change of hearts. Such a conversion, when it becomes the expression of a *life* of faith and not just of a *belief* in faith, goes through people like a shock, reaching deep down into the direction their lives are taking, into their established systems of needs and desires. It damages and disrupts our immediate self-interest and aims at a fundamental reorganization of our habitual way of life. The food that nourishes this revolutionary conversion is the "bread of life."

This anthropological revolution could be called our Christian reaction to the so-called crisis of survival. It is our attempt to achieve a new relationship to ourselves, to our natural and social environment, which is not one of domination and exploitation. It is our intrinsic contribution to ecology, and its inspiration comes from the heart of our eucharistic community. But this revolution, this struggle against ourselves, against our dominating-exploiting identity, is simultaneously and indivisibly the fundamental praxis of our solidarity with the poor and exploited peoples of this earth. Their poverty and our wealth, their powerlessness and our predominance, are bound together in a relationship of dependency. Hence, in the same way, the will to freedom of these peoples corresponds in our own situation to our struggle with ourselves, the struggle against the ingrained ideals of "always having more," against the total penetration of our entire biosphere by domination and competition. Only where this social dialectic proper to the ecological question is kept in view, will the struggle for survival waged on its behalf among us today avoid becoming a last attempt to save ourselves by burdening those who are already weak and oppressed.

This revolution may well be branded by some as inadequate, and by others as transparent betrayal. Yet no one should underestimate its political and social significance. For every revolution conceived only in social and economic terms, however purposeful and strategically intelligent its beginnings may be among the oppressed and injured masses, will fail if, in its development, it does not risk this anthropological revolution. It will fail if it considers such a thing already attained or even rendered obsolete by the social revolution it has struggled for or is struggling toward. What this will lead to will be only a rearrangement and a new division of those relationships of subjugation and dependency. It will not become the power overcoming this life of domination, but rather the power accomplishing it. Nietzsche would then remain still the stronger force within Marx!

But how and where can this anthropological revolution and the political culture envisaged by it take on concrete form? Who can bring it into being?

Basic Communities as Bearers of the Anthropological Revolution

The dimensions of the crisis of survival in contemporary society are increasingly leading to a situation in which moral and pedagogical principles are being reinstated within politics, with politics and morality being thereby reunited in a new way. The meaning of life and the quality of life, the revision of priorities in life, the acceptance of limits within life, renunciation and ascesis, a change of hearts—all these are maxims of survival we hear today, and these and similar demands are emerging more and more within today's political vocabulary. Up till now they have remained rather diffuse, occasionally threatening, Cassandra-like, then once more summoning us with a moralistic and pedagogical undertone. Political demands thrust their way into the domain of individual morality and individual life-style. This is a symptom of vast importance. It shows in fact that the classical bourgeois distinction between public and private is in a new way open to discussion. Not, of course, open to dissolution (this would only be possible at the cost of the political negation of the individual), but certainly open to be shaped in a new way. This new configuration must obviously take place at the grass roots of society. This is, in fact, the place where political life with its new demands becomes a personal reality, and a personal feeling of involvement can itself become a political reality. It is the place where politics and morality can be reconciled again in a nontotalitarian fashion. This would thereby become the starting point for the anthropological revolution.

Of course, in the meantime a growing number of groups have emerged at the grass-roots level of society, groups seeking or already practicing alternative life-styles in response to the challenge posed by the question of survival. Among these are certainly quite a few escapists fleeing into an apolitical way of life, seeking a naïve counter-culture based on political innocence. But there are many others who are really combining their struggle for a new way of life, a new life-style, with political responsibility; they are working, so to speak, in everyday political life for a new configuration of the relationship between public and private concerns. Among these are yet other groups who "live differently" in terms of an explicitly Christian motivation. It would be important in my view to see in these various groups and initiatives not only the usual outsiders (who appear continually in every society and in every church), but also the heralds of a new political culture being experienced in a still highly diffuse form. If they remain alone, they will soon lose whatever narrow political potential they now possess, they will disintegrate and be absorbed again by that total societal context of life which is the very thing needing to be transformed. Left by themselves, they are obviously incapable of being the bearers of the revolution we have been discussing.

But what would happen if our main churches themselves would at last take on more diversified forms at the grass-roots level? If they were to form of themselves something like basic communities, or at least allowed these more and more to exist, no longer viewing them simply as a product of the churches of the third world, as being nontransferable to us and specific to the third-world state of development? Such a development is blocked among us above all by the ideal of the "purely religious parish community." Yet the latter is, in far too massive a way, the organizational reflex of the church as bourgeois religion. It mirrors, in far too great a degree, the bourgeois distinction between public and private for it to be capable of contributing substantially to a transformation of this distinction. In addition, reasons of pastoral necessity have long since rationalized the ideal of the purely religious parish community. We hear time and again that the introduction of conflicts at the grass-roots level would only disturb the peace of the parish communities. As if community in the Lord's Supper made invisible the sufferings of society and the challenges this involves for those sharing in the eucharistic meal, when, in fact, it renders these realities uniquely visible.

In the meantime, the high price we are paying in our parish communities for this kind of social indifference and pretended political neutrality becomes ever more clear. All too often, by the avoidance of social differences and the ironing out of grass-roots diversity, these communities show the very features they were meant to overcome: such as the alienation and lack of contact among the churchgoers themselves, about which we hear ever increasing complaints. Perhaps there lies waiting in this increasingly obvious crisis of our churches an opportunity for radical change in their understanding of parish community. Just as in the Latin American Church, the basic communities combine together prayer and political struggle, the Eucharist and work for liberation, so in our context basic communities could and should develop as the motive force and the manifestation of that anthropological revolution which is nourished by the power of the Eucharist.

Of course, even a basic-community church could itself never become the sole bearer of such an anthropological revolution. Christians would have to follow a path here with many others, with many unbelievers also, who seek this revolution from motives which are totally different from those of Christians. And they would all have to reckon with many setbacks and many defeats.

Yet will we, in fact, have enough time to embark on this anthropological revolution? Enough time for the interplay between new praxis and a revolutionary change of consciousness? Enough time to find a way forward—one which avoids disaster—in humanity's present crisis of survival? Have we not already been standing for ages with the water almost over our heads? This indeed seems to be the case. And that is why I am far from certain that we will have sufficient time. However, my final commentary on this will be a reference to Martin Luther—to the famous answer he gave when he was asked what he would do if he knew that tomorrow the world would end. He replied: "I would plant a tree in my garden."

In my opinion, that answer is neither the expression of a feeble resignation to fate, nor an attitude of apocalyptic gloating. It is rather the expression of the cold-bloodedness proper to Christian hope. Without the latter we will certainly not risk that anthropological revolution, for which we as Christians are strengthened by the bread of life.

For Further Reading

Berger, Peter L., et al. *The Homeless Mind: Modernization and Consciousness*. Random House, 1974.

Enzenberger, Hans Magnus. *The Sinking of the Titanic: A Poem*. Houghton Mifflin, 1980.

Fromm, Erich. *To Have or to Be?* Harper & Row, 1976.

Gorz, Andre. *Ecology As Politics*. South End Press, 1980.

Hellwig, Monika. *The Eucharist and the Hunger of the World*. Paulist, 1976.

Marcuse, Herbert. *Essay on Liberation*. Beacon, 1969.

Powers, Joseph M. *Eucharistic Theology*. Seabury, 1972.

Schumacher, E. F. *Small Is Beautiful: Economics As If People Mattered*. Harper and Row, 1976.

4.

Toward the Second Reformation
The Future of Christianity in a
Postbourgeois World

From the First to the Second Reformation

To speak about the Reformation and make it, not just an object of remembrance, but an object of hope, indeed an incentive to change—change for all of us, including myself as a Catholic—means one thing: we must bring that question and that awareness which inspired the Reformation into a relationship with the present age. In this regard, I want to propose to you a thesis about the future of Christianity in a postbourgeois society. I am aware that this thesis is highly controversial and is certain to be challenged. Yet to risk what is controversial and to become thereby, precisely as a theologian, open to attack remains, in my view, not the least significant part of the moral heritage of the Reformation. The thesis is as follows:

The Reformation was situated within the disappearance of the medieval feudal world and the emergence of the so-called bourgeois, or at first early bourgeois world. It ushered in that tremendously influential form of Christianity by which that same Christianity asserts itself historically within the bourgeois world. Even Catholicism is affected—at least indirectly—by this Reformation. In the end, the so-called Counter Reformation was itself determined by that against which it struggled. And it even assimilated at least partially those problems and contradictions brought by the bourgeoisie into Christianity and rooted in the fact that by degrees the bourgeois citizen became the "real" Christian subject. If we

use the terms "bourgeois" and "the bourgeois" in a purely historical way, then we are now situated—unless all appearances deceive—at the historical end point and turning point of this bourgeois world. Christianity now stands within the disappearance of
this bourgeois world and the dawning of a postbourgeois, postcap-
italistic world. In this world, Christianity will be able to preserve
and develop its historical identity only if, as a totality, it achieves
a second Reformation, which means it must succeed in eating, as
it were, a second time from the tree of Reformation knowledge.

The parting from a bourgeois world and the transition to a postbourgeois one—in which the European West and still less the
Christian West no longer stand at the center of things, and in which
late Western individualism is beginning to become an increasingly
marginal cultural phenomenon—is perhaps as yet only recognizable
in its advance signals and general contours, and it remains still full
of unanswered questions and dangers. The immobility of the major
world-political blocks creates, not a sense of stability but confusion
and a contagious consciousness of catastrophe. In this situation,
where feelings and forebodings emerge of one age passing away
and being replaced by another age marked by radical change, there
breaks through again in a new way the original Reformation question: How can we attain to grace?

Many theologians writing about the Reformation assure us now-
adays that Luther's famous fundamental question regarding a gracious God can scarcely be made intelligible to people today, let
alone communicated as relevant to their lives. This question is said
to belong to another, noncontemporary world. I do not share this
position at all. The heart of the Reformation's question—How can
we attain to grace?—is absolutely central to our most pressing concerns. Just look for a moment at the human person of today: a part
of this late bourgeois world of ours, stretched between doubt and
commitment, between apathy and a meager kind of love, between
ruthless self-assertion and a weak form of solidarity, confused and
more uncertain of himself than he was even a few generations ago.
So uncertain of himself is he that he is scarcely willing to become
his own descendant. And we are asked to believe that this person
cannot understand the cry for grace, the pressing question as to
whether and how grace can come to us? I do not accept that for a

moment. It is not the *fact* that Christianity concerns itself with grace and speaks of grace which makes it so alien to people today, so noncontemporary and removed from their lives; it is much more the *way* Christianity does these things. But how should we speak about grace? How should we seek it? What does it mean to eat a second time from the tree of Reformation knowledge? What would this be: a second Reformation within the revolutionary change ushering in a postbourgeois world?

This second Reformation concerns all Christians, is coming upon all of us, upon the two great churches of our Christianity. It would be, therefore, in this precise sense, ecumenical. The needs of the gospel and the world will not let us indulge ourselves much longer with our one-sided, half-lame versions of Christianity. Yet before I say something about the bearers of this second Reformation, I have to speak about its thematic meaning and future aims. In what follows, I want to describe these briefly in terms of a threefold struggle for grace:

> Invoking grace in the senses—the second Reformation, Protestant version.

> Invoking grace in freedom—the second Reformation, Catholic version.

> Invoking grace in politics—the second Reformation, world-political version.

If we take "reformation" in its literal sense as "restoration" of original relationships and connections, then we speak of this second Reformation as grace returning to the senses, grace returning to freedom, and grace returning to politics.

The Second Reformation

In what follows, I am able to present these three varieties of the second Reformation only in the form of ideal models. At the very beginning, then, I want to ask for your understanding if this account appears to you all too abbreviated, oversimplified, and too one-sided. Nothing of what is written here is meant in an unloving or nonfraternal way. Quite the contrary. Let me say that I am speaking here, not with the calculated politeness of a stranger but rather, if I may put it this way, with the concern and intense sympathy of a brother.

Invoking Grace in the Senses—
the Protestant Variety of the Second Reformation
Allow me to begin with a personal impression, one which is very subjective and "vulnerable." Taken as a whole, Protestantism is to my mind too detached from the senses. We do grace no honor if we elevate it into the realm of the invisible and nonsensible. We minimize grace when we snatch it away from the senses and thereby from the social suffering of humanity. The Reformation's fear of sin became, by gradual degrees, another kind of fear. I call this fear of contact—fear of contacting what is of the earth, of the senses, of that bodily-social life within which grace wishes to bestow itself upon us—that grace of the God who has shared our humanity and who raises the dead to life. I am certainly not making this observation in the pose of the well-versed Catholic know-all. For even if Catholicism may have retained more of that connectedness with the senses, more of that receptivity and sensitivity to the perceptual and earthbound dimensions of grace and the Christian mysteries, it has scarcely attained this at that level of freedom to which the sense-bound world has been raised through the gospel and also through the Reformation.

What causes this Protestant fear of contact? The Reformation is marked by the pathos of "pure doctrine." For reasons which are all too understandable, it opposes this pure doctrine to the apparently pagan sensuousness of the Renaissance Catholicism of the time. Protestantism rejected, therefore, all mediations, all alliances with earthly concerns, with the sensuous and material world. It suspected in them that evil compromise which betrays God and God's grace. And yet we should ask today (with Kierkegaard, for instance): Has the Reformation not achieved a kind of "overkill" in this area? Is "pure" a biblical category at all, or an authentically Christian one? And is this still the case when "pure" is put forward, not just as a corrective principle within Christianity but as a guiding principle of Christianity itself? When this happens, does not the category of "pure" reveal itself as something fundamentally idealistic, as bound up with a nervous, abstract, and nonsensual theoretical Christianity, a Christianity trying to convince us that grace is mediated through the Word alone and by that fact contains nothing to be looked upon, nothing to be touched, and above all nothing to be handled and dealt with? Was this not a miscalculation on the part of the Reformation when it aimed at awakening the invocation of grace and the reform of the church solely through the Word and through "pure doctrine" instead of through real people and their sense-bound, anguished praxis, a praxis which the Reformation banished again all too quickly into its own private sphere? But it is exactly this dimension of praxis (and not that of the dogmatic comparison of confessional formulations separated from human beings and their praxis) which is aimed at by that movement of reform I am here calling the second Reformation.

Allow me first of all to name in a symptomatic and brief fashion some of the fears of contact and of adulteration. In my view, these include fears related to everything natural, to what is "pagan"—as if the festive joys of the senses were outside grace, and only the strained and often simulated joy of the spirit were truly engraced. Other fears are those related to impure, contradictory social conflicts—as if that grace which is alone decisive were to be experienced outside the senses, outside society, beyond the bodily-social existence natural to human beings. (This does not mean I am trying to approve the crude way we Catholics go around interfering in everything!) There are fears related to what are called material necessities, to the biological particularities of life and of life's sufferings—as if the mysteries of Christianity were not eternally bound up with this earth in a different and more radical way, certainly also in a more threatened way, than in all other religions. There are, finally, fears related to what people usually call "religion." If Protestantism could ever trust itself to be a religion, how powerful a religion it would be! It is, in fact, surely the only religion in the world which, through the voice of its theologians, proclaims that it in no way wishes to be a religion, that it is "faith alone," "grace alone,"—as if visible religion, festive religion, religion with liturgies based on contact and accompanied by the delight in symbols and myths did not comprise an essential, though always threatened, praise of grace present within the senses.

These fears have meanwhile begun their domination over modern Christianity, and strengthend their position by means of an enlightened bourgeois-idealistic theology. This theology is in my view nothing other than the theoretical expression of these quasi-constitutional fears of contact. By referring to its own scientific character, which forces everything related to the senses and, above all, everything practical to remain exterior and peripheral, this bourgeois-idealistic theology conceals its own irrational core.

We should spare ourselves the objection that this fear of contact is no more than a completely incidental and indeed purely psychological description of Protestantism. For impelled by this fear, there has developed over the centuries an historically powerful bourgeois Christianity marked by a dualism between the world of grace and the world of the senses. There has developed a graceless form of humanity, strictly oriented to property, competition, and success, with grace overarching the whole. In any case, this seems to me, even in the exaggerated ideal form I am describing, to be the basic configuration of Christianity as bourgeois religion in the way it has emerged within recent centuries—emerging also within Middle European Catholicism, although with a corresponding delay in time. In this bourgeois religion, it is possible to interpret all the central sayings of the New Testament, above all those of the Sermon on the Mount and the famous statements of reversal, in a purely spiritual fashion, as pure statements about interior attitudes: "The last will be first, but the first will be last." "Whoever wants to possess his life, will lose it; whoever surrenders it, will gain it. . . ."

In the biblical narratives and events, grace is encountered as a sense-related, historical-social experience. It is encountered in stories of awakening and exodus, of conversion and liberation, of discipleship, and of faces lifted up in hope. These stories are not additional embellishments upon an invisible event of grace; not at all. In them grace itself comes to expression, for example, within the historical-social life of a people in exile, in the experiences of discipleship undergone by a young community, of resistance to the representatives of Rome's political religion, or of solidarity with the least of the brethren. In all this, grace is being "seen"; it is a visible and sense-related grace. "Who sees his brother, sees his God" is a saying of Jesus handed down to us outside the canonical tradition. It sounds authentic, since it resembles another saying familiar to us all, that word from the Last Judgment according to which Jesus himself wills to be seen in the least of the brethren, even though we are obviously overlooking this continually: "But when, Lord, did we ever see you, see you naked, or see you hungry, or see you in prison?" When did we ever see you? And we are meant to believe there is nothing to see there, nothing to get hold of, nothing to touch? And is grace supposed to have nothing to do with the eyes, nothing to do with the hands? Are only the ears meant to be engraced, to receive the Word? Is everything else "profane"? Is it only the space where we apply Christianity, but not the place where we experience its grace?

Jesus obviously stakes everything on visibility, on decisive action to make visible, tangible, and imaginable the way people suffer and the causes of this suffering. We, on the other hand, stake everything on invisibility. Grace has to be invisible. Is that really the case? If nothing at all can be seen of a reality, that reality cannot be truly invisible either—invisible in the sense that it awakens the embodied pain expressing our hope. If nothing at all can be touched of a reality, that reality cannot ultimately be intangible either—intangible in the sense of drawing to itself the passion of our yearning. All too pervasively is our bourgeois Christianity founded on invisibility, on noninterference, on nontouching, on dualism. And we have long since become masters in the art of making invisible. The privileged experiences of Christ's visibility —his encounters with the poor and unfortunate, the excluded and humiliated: Are these really at the center of our so-called "religious experiences"? Are not all of us, both Protestants and Catholics, eagerly involved in taking just these anguished divisions between the rich and the poor, between the fortunate and the unfortunate, between the successful and the defeated, between . . . between . . . between . . . , and making them invisible? Above all, invisible there where we gather together in the name of Christ? What kind of grace accompanies us in all this? Do we, in the end, call grace invisible, so that our own sin should remain invisible? But is this kind of invisibility of God and of God's grace not destroying our own selves, as Bonhoeffer already surmised in 1932?

Our bourgeois Christianity is sickening from a sweet poison, the poison of a mere belief in faith and in the praxis of discipleship, a mere belief in love and repentance. All grace remains thereby in the realm of invisibility and intangibility. And we ourselves remain always unchanged, we go on defining ourselves by the trusted standards of our bourgeois identity. Grace in this case is not the grace given to us or promised us by God, but the "graciousness" we bestow upon ourselves, the grace without consolation typical of bourgeois religion—"cheap grace," as Bonhoeffer called it. A grace that does not penetrate or assail our lives, but just overarches our earthly-social life, totally separated from the senses, invisible and intangible, and precisely as such becoming the seal of our hopelessness and not the firstfruits of our manifold consolation. Christianity as bourgeois religion does not console.

The second Reformation would, therefore, still be concerned with the pressing question as to how we could receive grace and consolation. It aims thereby at the sensuous-practical core of grace, at the discovery of "costly grace"—to cite Bonhoeffer once again—knowing that it is not in our power to separate this from our sense-related experience in society and politics. Yet the very fact that every sensuous praxis of grace, without which no mysticism of grace can exist, at once attracts our suspicion as being negative politicization or banal actionism shows clearly how far removed we are from any return of the senses into the world of grace. So we prowl around in a circle of banal materialism which we cannot escape even when we cover it over, in the fashion of bourgeois religion, with the mysteries and with grace representing invisible values.

Thus the invocation of grace in the senses and within the sensuous praxis of our lives signifies essentially the separation from our bourgeois Christianity inasmuch as it is built upon the dualism between invisible grace and a graceless humanity dependent on works. Moreover, too long have we related such dualism between the world of grace and that of the senses to the individual alone. In fact this has a social history also. For this kind of dualism reinforces oppression, and allows grace to appear only too easily as something covering over an unliberated sensuous-social world marked by unredeemed powers of domination. The second Reformation protests, therefore, against the domination of invisible grace. Without sense-related struggle, it acknowledges no mysticism of grace and aims, therefore, at a Christianity beyond bourgeois religion, to be attained through the invocation of grace in our social life, in our life of the senses.

Invoking Grace in Freedom—the Catholic Variety of the Second Reformation

Catholicism has evidently preserved a particular insight into the condition of the so-called enlightened human being of today, this extremely nonsensuous person, with his very nonmysterious cult of an exclusively dominating relationship to the world, with his abstract seizing of power over nature. In the name of grace, such a person ought not to be made even less connected to the senses than he is already. Catholicism, therefore, holds firmly to the insight that we cannot remove the senses from grace without obscuring or even destroying the presence of grace itself. Catholicism does indeed know something like a Manichean hatred of the senses, but not that ignoring of the senses which is found in Puritanism. Yet Catholicism's connectedness with the senses appears in fact to be insufficiently imbued with the yeast of freedom, that freedom of God's children. Just as we find in Protestantism a kind of constitutional suspicion regarding our connectedness to the senses, to the visible and representational dimension of grace—in brief to what is called the incarnational principle—so we find in Catholicism a kind of constitutional suspicion regarding grace as freedom. This is why the sense-related dimension in Catholicism often appears so reified, so distorted by sacramentalism and ritualism, so monolithic and regimented—as if the human being is no longer present there at all in his spontaneity and freedom.

In addition to this, Catholicism obviously has a very broken relationship to the bourgeois history of freedom of the modern era. The so-called "Catholic Ages" within this historical process were always—at least within our Middle European cultural area—ages for being "counter" or "against" this history of freedom. The recent Vatican Council appeared as the first embryonic opening of the church to these traditions of freedom, recognizing them initially at least as representing ecclesial elements of the freedom of God's children, elements rooted in the gospel itself: such a development can be seen in the Council's Declarations on Freedom of Conscience and on Religious Freedom.

Yet how are we to evaluate this whole historical process within Catholicism? Are we Catholics after all nothing but notorious late-developers in the areas of bourgeois freedom within Christianity and church? Is the Catholic resistance to this history of freedom and the noncontemporaneity of Catholicism regarding this history only mere backwardness? Do we, in the end, have any alternative to just assimilating—with all the patience and courage we can muster—the first Reformation with its evidences of freedom, as our own progressive theology is trying to teach us? Or could there perhaps be something like Catholicism's own reformation situation whereby it would make its jump forward, its own leap into the freedom of God's children? To my mind, the answer is in the affirmative, and I would like to elaborate and clarify this opinion further, since it lies in the direction of the Catholic variety of the second Reformation.

The Protestant model of the invocation and discovery of grace in freedom is familiar to us all, being spread out before us in the history of the Reformation up to the present day. It involves the freedom of the individual person who, in the presence of his gracious God, is no one's slave and servant. As we know, this "freedom of the Christian person" led also, in a highly complex causal interplay, to the political freedom of the bourgeois citizen. Alongside this, another model of the Christian attainment of freedom and of the discovery of grace as freedom appears to me possible. Perhaps, in a future ecumenical Christianity, it will be named the Catholic model. What do I mean by this? What we are concerned with here is the Christian experience of freedom as *liberation*. We are dealing with that process in which the individual experiences himself, not in isolation but in the solidarity of community, free in the presence of his God. In this process, it is "a people" which becomes free, experiences itself as called forth and liberated to become the subject of its own history in the presence of its God. It is not the isolated history of freedom of the individual which is in the foreground here, but a history of liberation in solidarity—the coming-to-be of a "people" as subject and, naturally and necessarily within this, the coming-to-be as subjects of individuals also.

The gospel itself contains more than only the Pauline model of the Christian attainment of freedom, which is the primary reference point of the Reformation. Besides this, the gospel presents us with a synoptic model of the Christian attainment of freedom. I am thinking of Jesus who liberates "the people" to become a "new people," not by appealing to it on a populist and mass level but by summoning it and calling it forth out of its archaic fears and tabus. It could perhaps be said therefore, in an extremely undifferentiated reduction, that the gospel itself already manifests two strands of the attainment of freedom, which admittedly must remain always intertwined: one strand is more individualist and liberalist in orientation, the other could perhaps be called more socialist—with all the reservations accompanying that designation.

If we understand the reformational invocation of grace in freedom as the invocation of grace in liberation, then must we not say that, for Catholicism today, its reformational hour of freedom has struck? After all, we are seeing manifested precisely within the worldwide Catholic Church the beginnings of such an invocation of grace in the liberation of poor and oppressed human beings and peoples. I am referring to the basic-community churches of liberation and also to the theology of liberation in the poor countries of the world, above all—in the context of Catholicism—to the Latin American church. In this church, energetic attempts are being made to bind together the ideas of redemption with those of liberation, and to live out and proclaim this emerging configuration of freedom as a precious heritage of the gospel. Of course, everything will depend on whether Catholicism in our countries, in the wealthy countries of this earth, is prepared to recognize the providential reformational mission of the poor churches for the whole church and for the whole of Christianity. And whether it is ready to allow into the heart of the church the forward thrust of this understanding of freedom, and not put barriers in its way with the objection that this is at most a specifically developmental form of expression in the so-called "underdeveloped" countries—or to even call it a betrayal of the Christian heritage of grace.

We can say with certainty that this second Reformation would come neither from Wittenberg nor from Rome. It would in no way come upon us from out of Christian-Western Europe; instead it will come out of the liberation Christianity of the poor churches of this world.

Yet what do these poor churches really mean to us, these churches in which, tenaciously and not without great difficulties, a new Christian experience of freedom is beginning to prevail? Do they really signify for us something other than the object of our occasional charitable compassion which comes into operation mostly around the Advent and Christmas seasons? Do they truly represent for us a providential situation in which grace is coming to all of us? Are they, for us, the church of a Catholic Reformation? I have nothing against giving money to these poor churches, provided we do not thereby forget that this money renders invisible to us the sufferings and struggles in which *they* are experiencing grace. I do not object to the help we give them, provided we realize that this is not everything, and certainly not the most essential thing that unites us with them. The most essential thing would be the awareness that out of these poor churches a reformational impulse seeks to come upon us all.

It is true that the general atmosphere in the church seems unfavorable for such a prognosis. The basic-community churches of liberation are generally regarded with scepticism, if not with actual mistrust and rejection. Anyone who makes this an issue, anyone attempting to force this connection between grace and liberation onto the agenda of the whole church, experiences swift isolation and suspicion within the church. If my perception is correct and I am not judging too hastily, then the Catholic Church to which I belong, under its present pope, is seeking vigorously to regain and strengthen anew its basic Western and European orientation. In recent years, under the pontificates of John XXIII and Paul VI, it appeared as though the Roman Church was developing a growing awareness of the significance of these poor churches for the whole church and indeed for the whole of Christianity. The theological and pastorial priorities in Rome appeared to be undergoing a cautious yet unmistakable change.

Today, however, I see the tendency being clearly reversed. This comes to expression not least in the priorities established by the present pope within his pastoral and magisterial concerns. This reversal may be welcomed here and elsewhere, and may have been so desired from the beginning. The danger I see in this—and I may be allowed at the present time to say this openly—is that our Catholic Church could miss its reformational opportunity, wherein it makes *its own* experience of freedom in the experience of grace as liberation. Through this experience of freedom, it would at last find greater access to that freedom of Christians achieved in Protestantism. The Catholic Church would thereby see in the call for rights to freedom within the church, and in the call for repentance addressed to church authorities and institutions, not simply liberalistic tendencies toward self-dissolution. It would recognize instead that protest which the gospel itself proclaims against the actual state of the church's life.

Invoking Grace in Politics—the Political Variety of the Second Reformation

This insistence on grace in the senses, and on grace in liberation is an insistence on grace in political life. Yet, is grace in politics even possible? Ought such a thing to exist? Is not the very life of modern politics their intrinsic lack of grace, known everywhere today as the laws of practical politics? Politics under grace instead of under the constraints of the issues: Is such a thing not, at best, a harmless and naïve expectation? Does it not conjure up, at worst, a confusion between religion and politics we thought we had long since left behind?

Yet this demands a very close scrutiny! What are these issues, these means in political life today, for which politics usually declares itself competent? If we look closely, we see that today for the first time this no longer involves just one or another issue, one or another means. Instead, it involves the end itself; that is, it involves human beings themselves and the new relationship they must attain toward themselves and all others, as well as to their social and natural environment. Man himself is at stake in politics, and it is this very fact that makes our usual kind of politics—which values grace little and issues a great deal—so confused; indeed, this makes many people tired of political life itself. Yet what does that mean—man himself is at stake in politics? All the major social, economic, and ecological questions can be resolved today only through fundamental changes among ourselves and in ourselves, through a kind of anthropological revolution. The issue today—and this applies in a special way to politics also—is that we should learn to "live differently," so that others should be able to live at all.

Living differently: this was indeed always a characteristic mark of Christians. And when Christians truly believe in grace, in its free and liberating presence, in its intimate connection with our senses, then it must also mean that in society as well they do not just live under the anonymous constraints of the issues, but under the "constraint" of grace. But grace signifies here the ability to interrupt, to stop; it means not simply having to go on living as before. Grace is the capacity, manifested at last in the political dimension also, not to see ourselves and evaluate ourselves with our own eyes but with the eyes of our victims, out of which, in the end—the Lord himself impressed this on us with unmistakable clarity—he himself looks upon us.

And it is precisely this change of viewpoint, this kind of interruption, this refusal to allow things to keep going on as before—in short this act of resistance toward ourselves and our way of life till now—that are at stake in politics today. With the ingrained humanism of expediency determining our politics, and with the graceless morals of expediency permeating our bourgeois life, we will be unable to make progress in our present situation. The question thus emerges here again, in the midst of our political life, as to whether we, once more, can attain to grace. This would be a grace which does not indulgently spare us but extricates us from these supposedly unavoidable constraints. This grace ultimately makes possible for us a new life of solidarity, a life which is no longer dependent upon the oppression of others. Such a grace passionately resists that form of solidarity which is systematically distorted by mass uniformity or hatred, without, at the same time, rejecting that new solidarity which unconditionally demands that we enforce our own social identity, not in opposition to weaker groups and classes which are deprived of social and economic power, but rather in solidarity with them.

When Christians in this political situation invoke that costly grace, with its sense-related dimension and liberating power, then by that very fact they are taking part in an historical struggle that has long been raging, a struggle for a world threatened by global social oppositions and ecological disasters, a struggle for a post-bourgeois, postcapitalist world, and what amounts to a postbourgeois humanity. Perhaps it also depends precisely on Christians as to whether the bourgeois finds an historical successor, someone to inherit the freedoms he has fought for so arduously. Without these freedoms any political culture expressing the new life of solidarity—that is, any such culture worthy of the name—is indeed unthinkable. It is true that Christians can only put forward this return of grace to politics in a credible fashion when they overcome in themselves that form of Christianity which I have described at the beginning as purely bourgeois religion. Both varieties of the second Reformation—the Protestant one in the direction of allowing grace to penetrate the senses, as well as the possible Catholic one oriented to a gradual discovery of the liberating character of grace—aim finally at this kind of Christianity beyond bourgeois religion.

Bearers of the Second Reformation

Who are the bearers of this second Reformation? It clearly emerges from what has been said till now that in both the major churches scarcely any basis exists in the masses for a second Reformation. Yet we must emphasize at once this other fact: that such a Reformation is not primarily the task of great individual reformers. Its main representatives are not individual religious leaders, nor even political leaders, nor are they outstanding theologians or church dignitaries; they are not individual prophets or saints either. If my view is correct, this second Reformation is the true "Reformation from below," what we might call the "grass-roots Reformation." It will not come upon us as a dramatic individual event; it is much more an unobtrusive and protracted process—tenacious, and accompanied by numerous setbacks and deepseated irritations.

Nor do I believe that the traditional parish communities in the church can be the main bearers of this reformational process—at least not in this country, where the dominant ideal is that of the "purely religious parish community." This is itself in too great a degree the organizational reflex of bourgeois religion—that same bourgeois religion which this reformational process aims gradually yet decisively to overcome.

In this context, I wish once more to bring to our attention—especially in regard to my own church, but not to it alone, the poor churches of the third world. In those churches, in fact—although under special conditions which are not simply transferable so as to have the same meaning elsewhere—the bearers of this reformational process are apparent. What have been called basic communities have developed there. In their central forms of life, these communities are seeking from below, from the grass-roots level of church and society, to bind together mysticism and politics, religious and societal praxis, and to assimilate into their eucharistic table fellowship the fundamental social conflicts and sufferings surrounding them. Thus Christians are ceasing to be objects of paternalistic care in church and in society, and are becoming the subjects of their own religious-political history.

This, in my view, is the precondition for a genuine reformational (and not just reformist) process in Christianity today. For such a reformational act does not take place today, as it did in Luther's time, on the basis of a unified Christian world. Nor does it happen any longer within the context of a society with an unquestioned religious orientation. It happens instead within a society that is ideologically extremely multilevelled, and indeed antagonistic. For this reason, a process of reformation today must explicitly include also within itself its own societal context, and continually keep in view the situation of its own subjects within society. Only then can it avoid becoming sectarian or even totalitarian.

Admittedly, in my own country, these basic communities have not been held in very high esteem up till now. A certain approval may eventually be given to their value for the churches of the third world as part of their specific stage of development, with the understanding that they are not transferable. In our situation, the ideal of the "purely religious parish community" is to be clung to, since the peace of such a community would only be disturbed by the introduction of societal conflicts on a grass-roots level, as if grace made social sufferings and those affected by them unseen, and not—for the very first time—visible, and as if grace in some feeble fashion were to incorporate everything into itself and be nonpartisan! The parish communities in my own country are paying a high price for this kind of prescribed indifference toward society. They are, in fact, manifesting all too clearly those very features which their pretended social and political neutrality were intended to avoid, namely a particular kind of disconnectedness, an absence of real conflict and encounter, a frigidity, an alienation, a minimal power of attraction and identification, not least where young people are concerned. In addition to this, our main churches attempt to order their relationship to society along purely institutional lines, namely in the relationship between church and state, so that one often has the impression that our churches function like highly organized bureaucracies, like well-equipped apparatus, even when their base in society has long since disappeared.

I am, of course, not suggesting here that we should simply copy the basic communities as these are developing in the poor churches of the third world. Nevertheless, we will only arrive at this process of a second Reformation among us when our main churches themselves begin at last to take on a more diversified form at the grassroots level. That is, when they develop in their own situation something like basic communities, communities that are concentrated around the Lord's Supper, not organized around the principle of territoriality nor pretending to societal or political neutrality. Such basic communities would also be the embryonic cells of a new ecumenism. The energetic development of such basic communities are being prevented in my own country, not only by the prevailing church concordats which derive their inspiration much less from the ideal of church as basic community than from a kind of enlightened state church with the privileged status accorded to a great ecclesiastical institution.

If we want to hold on vigorously to the eucharistic center of these basic communities, then their development is hindered above all by those church ordinances relating to the whole church, ordinances prevailing in the Catholic Church today but in no way unchangeable in themselves. Examples of this would be the image of parish community in these ordinances, the criteria laid down in them for admission to ecclesiastical orders, above all the image of the community leader and presider at the Eucharist—in short the prevailing image of the priest. Properly speaking, the leader of such a basic community and the presider at their celebration of the Lord's Supper should be able to come forth out of that community itself. In my church, however, this model of priesthood is opposed by the obligation to celibacy enjoined on all priests, which as a general rule does not allow the priest to develop out of the basic community itself. Certainly the leaders and presiders of such a basic-community church should not need to have religion alone as their profession in society; they would have to be able to exercise a secular profession alongside their church ministry, something which is practically nonexistent among us, and appears scarcely to be desired. And many other aspects of this whole question would need to be discussed.

Will we therefore be able to arrive at the formation of this kind of basic-community church on a wide basis? Will those reformational impulses seeking to advance from the poor churches into the heart of the whole church be allowed to take effect here also? In the foreseeable future, this seems to me scarcely possible. Certainly, we must not underestimate the price we will have to pay for the reformational transition toward such a church as a basic community. It would, in fact, have to be paid by all, out of all our pockets, by the church leaders as well as by the whole church as a people.

I want to remind us, of course, once again that this second Reformation is more than ever a "Reformation from below." As such it has already begun; indeed it has begun in both churches. Its starting point cannot be given a fixed date. In truth, we could all become its bearers or its supporters. We have, in any case, enough there to sustain our hope. *"Spiritus Sanctus,"* I read once, *"nec scepticus est nec opportunus"*. A very free rendering of that would be: The Spirit of God is neither with the sceptics nor with the totally satisfied. It still blows where it wills, when it wills—yet, at the same time, only as long as it wills.

For Further Reading

Bloch, Ernst. *Atheism in Christianity*. Herder and Herder, 1972.
"Does Our Church Need a New Reformation? An Orthodox Reply (A. Kokkinakis), A Protestant Reply (H. Roux), An Anglican Reply (S. Neill), A Catholic Reply

(J. B. Metz)." In Hans Küng, ed. *Post-Ecumenical Christianity* (=*Concilium* 54). Herder and Herder, 1970.

Fromm, Erich. *Escape from Freedom*. Holt, Rinehart and Winston, 1963.

Jaspers, Karl. *The Origin and Goal of History*. Repr. Greenwood, 1976.

Moltmann, Jürgen. *The Future of Creation: Collected Essays*. Fortress, 1979.

Plessner, Helmuth. *Laughing and Crying: A Study of the Limits of Human Behavior*. Northwestern University Press, 1970.

Tracy, David, et al., eds. *Toward Vatican III: The Work That Needs to be Done*. Seabury, 1978.

5.

Christianity and Politics
Beyond Bourgeois Religion

"Confront Fears—Confirm Hopes"*: This theme would do honor to any Evangelical or Catholic Congress. In any case it allows me, as a theologian, the opportunity to remain within my theological competence without mistaking the political theme I am addressing here.

In what follows, I am not concerned with political casuistry, with the question, for example, of how churches and political parties can cooperate more successfully in individual areas within the existing structure of politics with its so-called practical constraints. My theme here is the ability of politics and religion to enter into coalition and alliance with each other in developing new political perspectives, and in considering fundamental changes within our political life. I am, therefore, concerned, not with actual political administration and its necessity, but with what politics does, or should do, to set new things in motion. I am seeking to offer a perspective, not a prepared formula. This perspective can indeed be relevant to everyday political life, and may even have significance for political elections, as long as the voters are not being underestimated according to the view that they only vote on the basis of

---

*This was the original title of the address I gave in response to an invitation from the study group called "The Churches and the Social Democratic Party in Bavaria" (see "List of Sources"). It differs, at least in regard to its circle of hearers, from the other talks assembled here. At the same time, its inclusion in this volume seemed to me meaningful and necessary since in it a number of viewpoints which can be regarded as typical of all these talks are here explicitly related to a political context.

formulas (which they usually do not trust anyway beyond election night), and not also on the basis of perspectives. At a time when—as is the case today—politics is unavoidably turning into world politics, within which, ultimately, our whole earthly fate is at stake, then such politics is also concerned with the presentation and the defense of something hoped for.

To see hope within politics seems like the revival of that permeation of religion and politics which has meanwhile become obsolete. Yet the clear and precise separation of religion and politics is itself politics, and in my view not the best kind, the kind that today is coming more and more from the right, even when it is put forward in liberal clothing. I am nonetheless convinced that the carousel of politics would be more inclined to move to the left if it were to turn to the melody of the gospel, especially the Sermon on the Mount. Admittedly, Bismarck already impressed upon the parties and churches in this country—and this lesson they have also followed more or less dutifully up to the present day—that, in fact, nobody can build a state with the Sermon on the Mount. So there is scarcely any danger that through the gospel we could be thrown politically out of our trusted step. But what if the political catastrophe were to consist precisely therein, that we just let everything go on as before?

Establishing the Situation: The End and Transformation of the Bourgeois Age

I shall begin with a brief overview of the situation, with a short description of the starting point for my theological-political reflections. This situational report cannot be purely analytical in character for the simple reason that the analysis of an historical situation never describes the present; it describes at best only the most immediate past. What I am attempting to say about the situation is necessarily anticipatory in character; it gesticulates, as it were, with the future in order to focus on the present and on present tendencies in as comprehensive a way as possible. This way of ascertaining a situation remains, of course, always controversial: it is necessarily hypothetical in scope. Its objectivity resides not least in the fact that it allows for contradiction and correction.

If I see things correctly, we are now living within the final phase, which is also the transitional phase, of an historical period. Precisely because this period is approaching its end, it can be understood, grasped, and characterized as a totality. It is that historical period which was shaped—in an extremely complex causal interplay, of course—by the Reformation and the bourgeois Enlightenment, and which we can, therefore, call the period of bourgeois society. The concept "bourgeois" and "the bourgeois" is being used here first of all in a purely historical sense, and in this sense I believe we can say that we are living within the historical end point and turning point of what has been called the bourgeois world.

There are, in fact, today a vast number of what can be called characterizations of "the end"; at least indirectly all of them seem to me to point to that historical process I have just indicated. Many years ago, for example, Romano Guardini already spoke about "the end of modern times"; much discussion was aroused by Arnold Gehlen's diagnosis of the "end of modernity" and the emergence of "post-history." Very recently, another conservative philosopher and sociologist, Robert Spaemann, put forward a thesis regarding the "end of modern consciousness." Yet these and similar characterizations of "the end" seem to me to remain too undetermined, in both a theological and political sense. They are much more difficult to grasp because they fail to discuss directly the questions: Who is the *historical subject* of this end situation? and what processes of historical transition and revolutionary change are emerging within it?

For was it not precisely the bourgeois who became the historical bearer of that modern age which figures in all these characterizations? Was it not the bourgeois who stood at the dawning of this so-called modernity?—the bourgeois whose historical enthronement was accomplished by means of the Enlightenment and the French Revolution, a process not without that quasi-messianic glory which such enthronements tend to take upon themselves. In fact, time and again the emergence of a new historical subject seems invested with this kind of glory. Are they not celebrating today in the countries of so-called objectively existing socialism the emergence of a "new human being"? Yet which of us would now be ready—without fear and without contradiction—to recognize in this new human being the new postbourgeois subject? Is not the ominous formulation of Theodor Adorno apposite here: "The horror is that the bourgeois found no successor."? And precisely for this reason, the struggle for humanity on the threshhold of a postbourgeois world appears to me so dramatic and conflict-laden, both theologically and politically. This is also the reason why the emerging departure from a bourgeois world, this transition, in fact, to a postbourgeois world, is accompanied by uncertainty and fear and by a latent sense of catastrophe that is eating at the souls of people in our first world.

In this situation, in which departure and radical change are being experienced or prophesied, fear and hope become once more politically relevant categories. Religion and politics enter into a new constellation with each other, one that can no longer be described in the "liberal" distinction between the two that is current among us. If we are to achieve a postbourgeois and postindividualist "rescue of the human subject," religion seems to me to be indispensable. Without religion, I see the barbarism of a blind negation of the individual breaking out within a postbourgeois society. Without religion, the end of bourgeois society threatens to become the very "end of the human subject."

I now owe you a more precise description of the symptoms marking this situation of departure and upheaval. General indications of it are already being discussed today even in our mass dailies: the atomic threat, the arms race madness, the destruction of the environment, the scarcity of resources, the crises of growth, the almost unmanageable dialectic between ecology and economy, the spread of terror, and above all, the threat of a global struggle for resources in what is called the North-South conflict.

In our own country, we would know more about this "end" if we ourselves—once again in a theological and political sense—had let the Holocaust be for us that "end" which it really was. We would then know more clearly that the period of historical timelessness and fatelessness of our bourgeois society (all dominant historical subjects imagine "their" time to be limitless in tendency!) had already reached its end. Yet we are obviously not only a "belated nation," but we were also late, too late, in attempting to raise ourselves up above the Holocaust by means of an unbroken ideal of progress. How could it be otherwise that precisely in this country the sensitivity to this historical situation of upheaval is less developed than in other countries?

Yet I want here to bring out especially one symptom of this upheaval, since it seems to me to be both theologically and politically explosive in its potential. I am referring to the irrevocable entry of the third world into our socio-economic, political, and theological situation. This new situation and the challenges accompanying it must be kept by us constantly in mind, both in the theological and political sense, so that peace may remain a political and moral possibility.

It is therefore demanded by political realism that we should strip the situation in this country of its tactical provincialism and understand it as an integral part of a single political world situation. This is no escape into irrelevant political abstraction. What is abstract today is much more that political point of view which "abstracts" from the worldwide entanglements and dependencies in which our own political life is ensnared. It is this point of view, to take one example, that sees in the countries of the third and fourth world only our weakly developed partners but not our victims. And it hopes to bridge over the oppositions that have broken out between the poor and the rich by employing a smoothly flowing concept of development, thereby avoiding the need for decisive changes among us in our first world. Apathy would then be the foundation of our political objectivity. But this leads in the end only to that kind of self-assertion which is empty of reflection and devoid of vision. It does not lead into the political and moral shaping of peace.

Conversion of Hearts: Theological and Political Dimensions

My starting assumption is that this kind of peace will only be possible when, in the predominantly rich countries of this earth, in the so-called first world, we arrive at a decisive revision of our priorities in life. This means that the objective fear and despair that are spreading throughout this first world of ours must become at last a living, personal experience. In other words, we ourselves have to search for and attain—in both a theological and political sense—a "conversion of hearts." This conversion is, of course, a central idea in the Bible. It describes, precisely in reference to the biblical awareness of humanity, an intervention within the total reality of the human situation. It signifies a radical revision of our life in the presence of God, one which may not be kept apart, in a dualistic fashion, from the contradictions of political and social life. After all, the human being in this situation who undertakes a radical revision of life, whose heart is to be changed here, is not a being existing outside history and society. It is therefore not inappropriate but in the very nature of things for a theologian to speak about the political significance of the "conversion of hearts" demanded today and to seek to indicate that such a conversion means, for us, something like a departure from the privileged situation of our first world—or, to put it another way, the departure from our bourgeois epoch.

But one thing must be seen clearly regarding this conversion of bourgeois hearts, this anthropological revolution in which the bourgeois of the first world are to be freed, not from their powerlessness but from their excess of power; not from their poverty but from their wealth; not from what they lack but from their form of total consumerism; not from their sufferings but from their apathy. Such a conversion is not yet politically acceptable among us within the limits of democratic politics. The individual on his own can do very little in this area; conversion, in the sense indicated here, can only be achieved together with others. Yet how can we arrive at this communitarian-political process? How can such a conversion become politically acceptable? In my view, this can happen when, for example, our churches take up these ideas with greater energy, ideas which are not yet politically acceptable, but which are nonetheless obviously related to the authentic message of our churches. Admittedly, this kind of political and moral pioneer work is somewhat foreign to the churches in this country. Yet precedents for this do exist, examples of the attempt to advance a kind of politics which cannot till now be undertaken by the professional politicians themselves. I am thinking, for example, of the preparatory work which was undertaken both by the Catholic and Protestant churches in this country, or at least by individual groups within them, so that reconciliation with Poland might become politically acceptable among us. Today, of course, the preparatory work to be done would be much more fundamental and conflict-laden. The ideas I am now seeking to put forward are to be understood in relation to this kind of political and cultural preparatory work.

Developments in Catholicism

I have a special purpose in addressing myself above all, in this context, to the situation of the Catholic Church itself. In our country, the Catholic Church certainly gives outsiders the impression of still being particularly monolithic, overinstitutionalized, determined more by regulation than by inspiration, and more by rigorism than by radicalism. In any case, in our bourgeois society Catholics are considered to be late-developers, simply slow in learning the lesson of bourgeois freedom. This is at once true and false. After all, it may be an instance of the "law" known to historians as the "Leap-Forward of Late-Developers." This can be illustrated through what I once called the possible "Einstein effect" among Catholics. I read in a biography of Einstein that on one occasion the great physicist was repeatedly asked how he had arrived at his revolutionary insights. It was probably related to what happened to him at school, Einstein tried to explain. Already at school he always learned everything more slowly than others, and found it more difficult than others to understand things. Later on he had greater difficulties with physics than his colleagues did, and therefore stayed with a problem much longer and more tenaciously, as if still playing with the same ball when everyone else had long since moved on to new games. His biographer commented here that, in fact, Einstein had evidently so many learning difficulties in his youth that he could be described, in a certain sense, as a legasthenic.

Are Catholics, then, legasthenics in the school of bourgeois enlightenment and progress? I don't mind, provided one is daring enough to allow the Einstein effect to apply to us also, and to interpret the peculiar noncontemporaneity of Catholicism, not as a mere backwardness devoid of promise for the future, but as a radical, indeed a revolutionizing, possibility of uniting ourselves with contemporary reality and its challenges.

In order to relate this challenge and this hope to our present question, I want to draw your attention to the embryonic beginnings of a new development within Catholicism, a development which ought not to be underestimated, especially in its political implications. By this I do not mean the belated emergence of a liberal Catholicism, which is either being celebrated among us at present as progressive, or opposed as unorthodox. In my view, this represents nothing but a Catholic variation—in fact a belated one—of bourgeois religion and bourgeois theology, and shows no really new perspectives either for the church or for politics: In fact, this is the new—this time the Catholic—version, in which our bourgeois society ratifies itself once more. Only at first glance does the inclusive language of this bourgeois-liberal theology and religion, with its language about "the human being" or "the Christian," disguise the fact that it is simply an integral element in the unquestioning self-stabilization of our society. In this sense it is nothing but the political religion of the bourgeois. In its total moralization of the contradictions in society—a moralization revealed in its typical language regarding the "greed of the rich," "the envy of the poor"—it declares the conditions in society to be "natural" and in this sense "unchangeable."

In doing this, such a theology removes from sight the sacrifices our prosperity demands from others. It is, therefore, in no way politically innocent, but becomes instead a kind of legitimization theology for our bourgeois society. As such, it may be perceived as progressive and liberating in the early-bourgeois or petty-bourgeois milieu of our Catholicism. In my opinion it does not touch at all the heart of the gospel and the historical challenge to our church and our society. In distinction to this, there is another kind of awareness already present in the Catholicism of this country, as well as among Christians in general at the grass-roots level. This is the emergence of a new consciousness of solidarity, a new fundamental political direction which, in its initial stages, could be described as "postbourgeois" (and indeed postcapitalist), yet does not aim toward a collectivistic levelling-down of human individuality and subjectivity in the Christian sense of these terms. Instead, what is being sought after in this radical awakening is a new, as it were, postbourgeois principle of individuation inspired essentially by the gospel. According to this principle even the poorest and most damaged individual remains higher in value than any total determination of societal and economic reality.

Moreover, Christians are convinced that this individuation cannot begin to exist without religion. But precisely because they do not simply identify bourgeois individualism with Christian subjectivity before God (as bourgeois religion does), they are able to enter into the historical struggle for a postbourgeois image of the human being. What does all this signify then for the Catholic Church in this country? The observations I am now about to put forward do not express the official policy of the church. They refer primarily to a change taking place among Catholics, and this change is happening (I say this without any polemical affect) at the grass-roots level of our Catholicism.

Catholicism, as World Church and within World Politics

I will remind you, to begin with, that the initial historical, social, and cultural situation in which Catholicism as a totality finds itself is extremely broad and laden with tension—to a much greater degree than we see reflected in the German Catholic Church or than is present in Protestantism. In any case, the explosive North-South conflict, that is, the class opposition (or class-related opposition) between the rich and poor countries of this earth cuts right through the center of the Catholic Church; for instance in the relationship of the churches of Central Europe and North America to the church of Latin America. In the end this could not fail to affect the consciousness and the basic political orientation of German Catholics. The Catholics in our country, who have long closed themselves off from a bourgeois society perceived as being fundamentally Protestant, are today adding new dimensions to their religious and political consciousness. They are acquiring an ever deeper understanding that their relationship to those who share the same eucharistic table in the poor countries of the third world cannot be appeased by occasional charitable measures to reduce disparity. Perspectives from the Sermon on the Mount are suddenly taking on a new value within their political awareness and political judgment.

German Catholics are gradually learning to see themselves and their own situation through the eyes of the poor peoples, which means through the eyes of the powerless, the oppressed, and the have-nots. They are becoming ever more clearly aware that the cry of these poor Christians contains a basic questioning of our Christian life in the first world, a questioning that aims toward our conversion and the revision of our life. With increasing clarity, they see the objective guilt in which our first world is living, and they are intensifying their efforts to let this guilt be personally experienced so that it might at last become politically effective and productive within society. They are learning, finally, to understand these poor churches in their injury *and* in their dignity; they are understanding that these poor countries are not simply underdeveloped but are the result of a devastation done to them as the victims of our European expansion. They are beginning to unmask as prejudice the established common sense among us whereby everything in our ecclesial world that does not meet the standards of Central European development has to be considered underdeveloped. Ever more clearly, they are seeing the potential for human and Christian inspiration that is present precisely within the social and cultural spectrum of what is "Catholic."

In this sense, the awareness at the grass-roots level of the Catholic Church appears to me—at least in its beginnings—to be broader and less provincial in orientation than the pragmatic political awareness within our society as a whole. It is also broader and richer in perspective than one would guess from the official, political picture of itself presented by the Catholic Church in this country.

There are, of course, numerous difficulties and obstacles preventing this impulse to conversion and renewal, which comes to us out of the worldwide ecclesial situation of Catholicism, from being effective on a large scale in the church in this country. Apart from the fact that the image of the church held by our church authorities and dominating our theology appears to me still too Eurocentric in orientation, I want, above all, to draw our attention to the following obstacle: More and more, Catholicism itself has become here a form of bourgeois religion in which "Christian values" arch over a bourgeois identity without really affecting it in terms of a possible transformation or a promised fulfillment. Under the cloak of a merely believed-in (but not lived) faith, bourgeois individualism thus establishes itself with its feebly developed capacity for solidarity with others. Christianity easily becomes the religious alibi for bourgeois innocence and the guarantee of a good conscience in a situation that really requires us to make the experience of guilt and failure in regard to these poor churches the very foundation of our everyday consciousness.

Nevertheless, the pressure by osmosis of the churches of the third world upon the Catholic Church in this country is growing. This is true, above all, for what is called the grass-roots level of the church, and within this context it affects the Christian bourgeois also, who in my opinion believes his Christianity is capable of more than it demands of him under its dominant form of bourgeois religion, and who is often simply confused rather than apathetic. Under this pressure of the poor churches, a new awareness is ripening among us, and this will be put to political account as well. Such awareness is aiming, in its first outlines, toward a free, postbourgeois society with a new world economic order. In an increasing number of cases, the Catholic bishops of the third world are presenting the biblical demand for justice in the form of an explicit critique of capitalism. And among ourselves also—unless all appearances deceive—the understanding is slowly growing that this kind of critique is indivisible; that is, it can only be practical on a global level of application, which means that it concerns us as well. In *this* sense, a "socialist inspiration" for political conscience is no longer simply foreign within our church, nor does it appear any longer as flatly anti-Christian.

Once again, I am saying this primarily with reference to the poor churches within the one Catholic Church in the world. There is developing among these the first beginnings of a nonbourgeois culture of Christian freedom, one which is not simply—as we generally like to insinuate—prebourgeois or potentially totalitarian. What is at issue is the attempt, deriving from Christian inspiration, to attain freedom in the form of a liberation shaped by solidarity. If this succeeds (and it certainly cannot succeed without the "conversion of hearts" on our side), then it will have an absolutely providential significance, not only politically, but also for the history of the church.

In order to bring this closer, I want to remind you of the peculiar dilemma of Catholicism in modern times. Catholicism in our country has not only failed to assimilate the bourgeois history of freedom, it has even fought against it all the way. The so-called "Cath-

olic Ages'' in modern European history were always ages for being
"counter" or "against." We had the Counter Reformation, the
Counter Revolution, the Counter Enlightenment, the ages of political Restoration and Romanticism. But if we are to see in this not
only historical inertia, blind refusal, and mere backwardness without hope or promise (and if we cannot assume that so sensitive a
social body as the Catholic Church could simply ''retrieve,'' without self-destruction, what it has been refusing to accept for the last
five hundred years), then, in the light of all this, we should and
must ask ourselves if the Catholic Church has not been given *another* situation and *another* hour of freedom in which it is uniting
itself with the challenges of the present age. I see this ''hour of
reformation'' emerging for Catholicism and for its way of uniting
the freedom of the gospel with the desire of humanity for liberation;
it is emerging within the poor churches. Of course, everything will
depend on whether Catholicism in our country and in the wealthy
countries of the world is prepared to recognize the providential mission of the poor churches for the universal church and ultimately
for the whole of Christianity, and is ready to allow into the heart
of the universal church the forward thrust of this understanding of
freedom.

A Plea for a New Political Culture

My assumption, of course, is that in our Central European society a politics which is socialist in inspiration can only be made
possible and responsible through democratic means. This would
take on the form of a democratic socialism which does not deny
the achievements of the bourgeois history of freedom, but rather is
heir to these in an historical dialectic, and precisely thereby saves
this indispensable bourgeois heritage. In any case, we are talking
about a politics with a recognized division of powers, oppositional
rights, freedom of expression, sovereignty of the people, and so
on.

Yet what do the political realities look like in this country? Allow me to express these in the form of a dilemma: At a time when
the universal Catholic Church is confronted with problems that are
leading it to affirm for the first time a politics which is socialist in
inspiration—so much so that this kind of political option is already

intimated in individual documents of the ordinary magisterium of bishops—we are experiencing here in Germany a social democracy which is downplaying its socialist traditions instead of developing them democratically, and is concealing these traditions all too diligently behind the constraints of everyday politics. I certainly do not wish to ignore these constraints of practical politics, nor am I trying to entice you into a political dreamworld. Yet if the perspective I have developed here is not totally mistaken, then it gives rise to most pressing questions. What inspiration is really being provided by your party, the Social Democrats, for that political culture so urgently needed today, in which freedom and socialism interpenetrate in a way productive for each of them? What is your party doing to make effective within our politics something like a new principle of solidarity, the kind of solidarity that in no way aims at the totalitarian negation of the individual, the bourgeois individual included, but seeks instead the kind of individuality that no longer achieves its aims *against* other, weaker, and underdeveloped classes and countries, but *together* with them? Is it then astounding that your party has to listen to the accusation of your political opponents that democratic socialism is really an empty word?

Many difficulties certainly stand in the way here—even beyond the constraints of everyday politics. These include elements of what has been called "German ideology," elements which hinder the development of such a new political culture. I have in mind, as an example of this, the quasi-constitutional fear of contact between culture and politics in this country. As a consequence of this, our idea of culture is virtually determined by its opposition to politics, which gets the name of "dirty business" to an extent seen nowhere else—despite the protest of significant cultural figures among us who nevertheless find themselves outside the mainstream. For example, Walter Dirks's formulation that politics is the new name for culture sounds repugnant to German ears—or at least incomprehensible. I am also aware of the fact that Germany is a country without a revolutionary history of freedom, that its history shows a disturbing surplus of political accommodation and a considerable deficit in the area of resistance. It is my belief that this historical evolution makes it particularly difficult for us to reach an awareness of the situation of the poor and oppressed peoples and of the possibilities of liberation emerging for them in that context. In our own struggle for a new political culture we must certainly reckon with this situation, and with much else besides. Yet the challenge remains, and time is pressing.

If my view is correct, your party is already paying a high price for allowing that utopian possibility present within it to be obscured, a utopia bound up with the expression "democratic socialism." Young people are disturbed at this, the same young people for whom politics must always contain an element of fascination, or to put it another way, must represent an unsatisfied longing. The real danger to your party does not come from the newly formed, ecological "Green Party," but rather from your own abandonment of everything utopian.

The power of remembrance may be a good thing for your party, as it is for Christians; the dangerous memory of your own beginnings and the inspiration behind these. This beginning cannot, of course, be copied in an uncritical way, but it should not be suppressed either. I am taking the liberty of saying this to you, both in regard to new developments in my own church as well as with reference to the youth of our country.

Excursus

Allow me finally to add here a brief excursus regarding the theological-political terminology and semantics of my address. In it I have made critical use of the terms "bourgeois" and "capitalist." This way of speaking is certainly not unproblematical in our situation—for instance, with reference to those language clichés prevailing in East Germany. The same would hold for the positive use I have made of expressions like "socialism" or "a politics socialist in inspiration." Here also the division of Germany continues to affect the depth structures of our political language and its semantics. Anyone in West Germany who makes a principle of criticizing capitalism, quickly comes under the general suspicion of being an accomplice of East Germany—just as anyone in East Germany who uses the word "socialism" in a way that is at variance with state socialism is quickly and erroneously marked out as an agent of a capitalist power. The threshold of tolerance on either side in this matter is extremely low, which has led us to an overcautious polit-

ical language. People want at all costs to avoid misunderstanding.
Yet the same fate seems to be befalling the political language that
befell the theological one: concepts that avoid all possible misunderstanding are almost always, at the same time, sterile. In both
cases, in politics as in religion, there exist words which are historically extremely loaded, and yet which should not be abandoned,
for they contain within themselves a store of memories and antici-
pated and imagined hopes. The semantic struggle which has to be
waged for these words is, in my opinion, an important element
within politics or within theology.

6.

Transforming a Dependent People
Toward a Basic-Community Church

How Does Basic Community Emerge in the Church? Or: Overcoming Bourgeois Unapproachability

1. Whether a renewal of our church will take place, in the direction of what I want tentatively to call a postbourgeois basic-community church, depends above all, and not as the final step, on ourselves. We should not be too fixatedly preoccupied with the danger of "repression from above." Have we not interiorized the paternalistic church to such an extent that we think everything connected with church renewal ultimately depends on one thing: on change happening to those who take care of us, which means above all the pope and the bishops? The fact is, a dependent people has to transform itself, and not just behave like a people being taken care of. This is how "basic community" emerges in the church.

To my mind, much of our usual criticism of the church is itself just another expression of the interiorized paternalistic church. Criticism, in fact, that is fixated to an inordinate extent on authority, and, if possible, on papal authority. As if the motto were: Everything would go better in the church if we only had a better pope. On the contrary! If things are to get better in the church, it will depend before everything else on ourselves. And where this awareness breaks through, basic community emerges in the church. Certainly this also means that we should believe ourselves—and not just the bearers of church authority—capable of a greater measure of the gospel and of Christianity. We should believe ourselves capable of this, and require it of ourselves. We should therefore overcome, at least within ourselves, that lack of repentance and self-criticism which we deplore in the church, especially in regard to the church hierarchy. In this way basic community emerges in the church.

2. We tell ourselves that we want to be, at last, a "mature church." But if we want to achieve this, we have to analyze the situation very carefully. What I can say to you about this, in all brevity, is not in the first place an attempt to win your applause; it is instead a challenge to serious reflection. Maturity is a great ideal of the bourgeois Enlightenment. This maturity brought with itself, of course, a radically new attitude toward religion, an attitude I would like to describe here as the *bourgeois unapproachability toward religion*. Religion does not lay claim to the bourgeois; instead, the bourgeois lays claim to religion. Religion does not transform society; rather, bourgeois society does not rest until religion fits in with itself and with what it considers reasonable. However, this unapproachability of the bourgeois toward religion is not simply identical with the Christian freedom of the gospel, just as the Christian subject is not the same as the bourgeois individual, and bourgeois individualism not the same as Christian existentialism.

I am emphasizing this (even though in a quite abbreviated form) because our attempts at church renewal are threatened by a danger which I have already sought to denounce on more than one occasion. It is the danger of transforming Christianity into bourgeois religion; more precisely, of trying to renew the church on a basis other than that of the gospel—on the basis, namely, of that bourgeois religion which may appear especially to latecomer Catholics like ourselves as being particularly "progressive" and even "liberating." Nevertheless, Christianity as bourgeois religion is not the religion of the gospel; it is rather the creation of the bourgeoisie and of bourgeois unapproachability in regard to religion. The bourgeois no longer allows religion to get at him, but he uses religion when he needs it. Thus he himself has created that "services church" which no longer offers people real consolation, and which for that very reason we have to fight with every means in our power. The bourgeois himself has stabilized on a new and less demanding level that same paternalistic dependency-creating church which was meant to be overcome.

We may not avoid such reflections as we struggle today for a mature Christianity and a mature church. We Catholics are late arrivals in this field to begin with. We are usually considered late developers in the areas of emancipation and the bourgeois history of freedom, the ones who catch on after everybody else, the legasthenics in the school of progress and enlightenment. Yet this need not be to our disadvantage once we recognize the "dialectic" of progress and enlightenment. We may still have the duty to "stay behind and catch up," but over and beyond this we have been given the possibility and the task of perceiving the contradictions hidden in the process of bourgeois Enlightenment. Once we do this, we are freed from the need to repeat them in a stereotyped way. Ours is the chance and the task of approaching the themes of the freedom and maturity of Christians in a deeper and more radical way than has been possible till now in the history of Christianity. And, in contrast to bourgeois individualism, our approach will be one of deeper solidarity.

Ultimately, this is also important for the ecumenical character of the church renewal we are seeking. We ought not to strive for ecumenism among Christians simply on the basis of bourgeois religion. In my opinion, this is precisely what we owe our Evangelical fellow Christians. Yet this question must at all costs be scrutinized closely. For the emergence of a bourgeois church within Catholicism and the belated variation we have developed of a liberal bourgeois theology appears to many as a guarantee and a promise for a progressive ecumenism. These developments seem to be the long awaited foundation for a promising coming together of Christians in our country. And yet questions arise as to the viability of this ecumenical foundation. We must ask: Is it really the gospel which is the measure of our reconciliation and our unity? Do we not ultimately have a duty precisely toward our Evangelical fellow Christians not simply to repeat in our own way the contradictions which they themselves have already experienced and suffered through in their own church life? In my view, ecumenism will only advance when both churches in our country take energetic steps out of the provincialism of bourgeois church life and meet the challenges of the world church and of world Christianity.

3. The transition from a paternalistic church "taking care of the people" to a mature church "of the people" does not come simply from above; in fact, it cannot come from above at all. I share Hans Küng's opinion that no violent revolution is threatening from below. But even a quiet revolution does not come from above! That should be our starting point. Besides this, we have to reckon here in Germany with something more, something I have already named a specific "German ideology." This is our typically German mania for authorization and legitimation, according to which only those things may be undertaken which have already received complete official blessing. We might illustrate this by recalling Lenin's malicious remark: "When German revolutionaries occupy a railway station, they first buy themselves platform tickets." If we apply this kind of mentality to our question, we are forced to say: In this direction, a basic-community church cannot be formed. And yet this is the very thing we would need, this power to form things from below. This is the issue, not direct confrontation with the authorities.

4. What I have been saying up to now does not mean that we have to found a new church. Religion and church have been handed down to us from afar; anyone trying to found them anew would create little more than a caricature. The central ideas of religion, the idea of God, of truth, and of so much more, are not ideas of the twentieth century and its dominant form of reason. These ideas, if we wish to cherish them, always need the power and the loyalty of our memory and our tradition. And far too much has already been thought through in our church in advance, piled up as an irreplaceable store of dangerous memories, for us simply to abandon them or totally transform them without thereby suffering the loss of our Christian identity. For this very reason, the church can and must be appreciated and challenged as a space containing possibilities for Christian existence, possibilities that are still very far from being exhausted or burnt out. This view of things

in no way renounces criticism of the church or of the pope—even though such a critique is not presented here primarily in the name of bourgeois demands for emancipation. Rather, as I will show in a moment, it is presented in the name of the poor and oppressed peoples and churches; for ultimately, it is only in this way that such a critique attains its liberating power and depth—liberating as well for us, the bourgeois of the first world and of the wealthy churches.

Paternalistic Church–Bourgeois Church–Basic-Community Church

1. This question of the church's future forces us to consider those images of the church concretely effective among us. I see, above all, three such images more or less in competition with each other. There is a people's church, a bourgeois church, and a basic-community church. Or, putting it more precisely, we have a pre-bourgeois paternalistic church, a bourgeois supply—or services—church, and a postbourgeois initiative-taking church. This threefold division accorded to images of the church corresponds, moreover, to the three types of theology dominant among us. First, there is classical theology, which is fundamentally shaped by neoscholastic positions and with a strong apologetic orientation on behalf of a people's, i.e., paternalistic, church looking after the people. Next we have the beginnings of a bourgeois-liberal theology which finds its church support in that process whereby Catholic Christianity in our country is itself increasingly taking on the form of bourgeois religion. This theology criticizes both the theory and praxis of church authority, and does this preeminently according to the standards of bourgeois freedom. Finally, there are the political theologies of liberation which bring into organic unity a productive critique of both church and society, aiming toward a basic-community church as "church of the people."

With reference to these three images of the church, the following brief considerations seem relevant concerning the church's future. The people's church as paternalistic church—taking care of the people—belongs to society's past, not to its future. Despite unmistakable achievements, it finds itself everywhere within a process of dissolution toward what could be called a bourgeois church, which is itself determined by the bourgeois attitude of unapproachability.

This bourgeois church, in the form of a supply or services church, is becoming to an ever greater extent the determining factor—in practice, if not as a norm—for our understanding of church. This could be called a belated variation of a particular Protestant form of church within Catholicism. At the same time, this bourgeois church has already passed its historical zenith, and in this sense its future in society already lies more behind than before it. To my mind, the tragedy of German Catholicism lies in its attempt to open itself to developments in society and church—to join up with these or assimilate them—just when these developments have also passed their historical zenith; when those who produced them—in particular the moving forces behind the Reformation and the bourgeois Enlightenment—have already recognized their inherent contradictions and have begun to overcome them.

In our own situation, within German Catholicism, the postbourgeois basic-community church scarcely exists at present, and its future is totally unknown. But the situation changes when our church ceases to be provincial in its ecclesial perspectives and enters into relationship with world Catholicism. There, the basic-community church is already an existing reality, one which is full of promise. Nor does anything allow us to relativize this form of church as being only a specific ecclesial expression of the churches of the so-called underdeveloped countries.

2. This distinction between the three images of church mentioned above has, for me, an inclusive meaning; that is, all three are capable of being church in the Catholic sense: it is ultimately a question here of a complex process in the gradual development of the church's future. This applies, above all, with regard to the subjects of this ecclesial reality. The church cannot dissolve its people and somehow choose for itself new members; the bearers and motive forces of the coming church do not fall from heaven; they are, in the first place, (though not exclusively) members of the church and the professing Christians of today. In this sense, even the critique of the bourgeois church is not a denunciation of the individual bourgeois Christian. On the contrary, this theological critique credits the Christian qua bourgeois of our first world with effectively valuing himself and his religion more than is reflected in the polit-

ical expression of bourgeois society and in the religious and Christian expression of bourgeois religion.

3. If this is to happen we must, however, at last break through the armor of bourgeois religion. We must see through and overcome the subconsciously ratified confusion prevailing among us between bourgeois unapproachability and evangelical freedom. Only then will we escape from the misery of Christianity as bourgeois religion. This bourgeois religion demands nothing, but it also fails utterly to console. God can indeed still be quoted in it, but no longer really adored. God's grace does not break in, cast down, or raise up: it simply overarches, as a "value," our bourgeois identity and becomes in this sense truly "cheap grace" (Bonhoeffer), that very graciousness which we bourgeois preeminently bestow upon ourselves. And so, just as our bourgeois society provides less and less material for dreaming and poetry, our bourgeois religion itself supplies scarcely anything for mysticism and adoration, for resistance and conversion. Wherever our churches make greater use of their powers of awareness and decision in order to withdraw from the provocation of being bourgeois religious institutions they open themselves to the future form of the church as basic community. This formation of basic-community churches would not simply stand in open opposition to every form of a people's church. In fact, it could signal the beginning of a people's church with a personal foundation; in other words the beginning of a people's church as a "church of the people." This would bring about that step forward mentioned explicitly in the German synod's document, "Our Hope"; this speaks of "a step forward from a church which seems protectionistic toward its people to one which is a living church of the people, with all knowing themselves involved, in their own way, in the fate of this church and in its public witness of hope."

This forward look toward the future of the church as a basic-community church is accompanied by a diagnosis both of our whole society and of the world church. Such a twofold diagnosis provides an orientation for the following reflections.

Basic-Community Church Within a Diagnosis of Society

1. The prognosis regarding the future of the church as basic community is supported and accompanied by a societal diagnosis which will certainly be the most controverted stage in the argument. According to this diagnosis, we are increasingly fixed within a situation of transition and radical change. This situation might be tentatively described as a departure from what could be called the bourgeois epoch, and the transition to a free, postbourgeois and postcapitalist society. The church as basic community would now have the opportunity, in the situation of transition, of functioning not as a late arrival on the scene, but rather as an advance herald of something new, and this would be essential if we are to resist in time the threatening barbarism of a postbourgeois epoch.

Faced with such a situation of radical change, it is precisely bourgeois individualism that seems to me least ready and capable of defending the legitimate achievements of the bourgeois history of freedom. This individualism, emerging as it did out of the Reformation, the Enlightenment, and the French Revolution, advanced the idea of the individual in so abstract and isolated a direction that the bourgeois individual who resulted is now capable of solidarity in only a weak and diminished form (despite or even because of the many emphatic protestations of solidarity). A senseless mechanism of self-assertion is totally useless here, as useless as the bourgeois "siege mentality." The only thing that can help is a conversion which reaches down to our very roots and incorporates into itself the economic foundations of our social life as well. What is also being demanded of us by this revolutionary situation is, therefore, not the bourgeois attitude of unapproachability which has led to the current "liberal" separation of religion and politics, but rather, in opposition to it, a new productive meeting of religion and politics. Only thus will a postbourgeois humanity emerge that involves neither the negation of the individual nor the undialectical rejection of the bourgeois history of freedom.

2. We can observe numerous signals of this coming radical change. In our own country, whenever we become aware of social-religious signs of crisis, we are necessarily reminded again and

again of the Holocaust. Then, more generally, we have to note the end of progress in the sense in which progress was shaped and formed in the bourgeois Enlightenment. There is the growing probability of disaster (and I say this without any apocalyptic gloating), a consciousness of limits and of catastrophe in our society; a consciousness, in fact, which is today shattering the peculiar timelessness of bourgeois society with its representation of time as an endless continuum of progress.

And yet, in my opinion, the most important signal heralding the above-mentioned radical change is the inescapable entry of the third world into our own historical and societal situation. Central Europe, comprising our bourgeoisie and Christianity, can no longer afford a world plan which it would construct via the model of smooth progressive development. To do this would simply unmask the arrogance of our Central European logic of development, which allows us to designate ourselves as the unquestioned summit of world evolution within society. Precisely through this entry of the third world into our own horizon of consciousness, we are experiencing with ever greater clarity that these so-called underdeveloped peoples are very often the victims of our European expansion. With increasing urgency, their misery is becoming a practical question interrogating our own bourgeois and Christian identity. It is becoming a challenge to judge ourselves—politically and as a church—through the eyes of these victims of ours.

3. In the light of this situation, our political life seems marked by what could be called a "tactical provincialism"; that is, we are seeking first of all to define our political and social identity independently of the poverty, misery, and oppression in the third world. Consciousness among us of the far-reaching structures of dependency between the first and third worlds and, connected with this, awareness of the objective guilt of our first world and the demand for radical conversion such guilt forces upon us—none of this seems as yet to be acceptable as practical politics in a democratic sense. A politician who established his priorities and directed his activity in accordance with this conversion would be removed tomorrow from the political arena. It is here that I see a provocation and a chance precisely for our church. Our church officials cannot be removed by simply being voted out of office. This should not,

of course, be understood as any kind of private privilege. It is rather a guarantee for, and an incentive to, high-risk activity, not only within the specific area of the church but in the political arena also. In this sense, for example, our bishops could function precisely in this area as an important pioneering force, and could help to make this conversion we need in the first world a political reality. It is already evident today that on this conversion world peace ultimately depends.

4. Now our bishops do indeed know something like a critique of bourgeois society (and also of bourgeois religion). With the power of the conservative imagination, they perceive the contradictions in this bourgeois society of ours. Everywhere they decry a so-called erosion of values. Nevertheless, in my view, their critique remains virtually truncated. For, in the long run, values can only be saved when we uncover the roots of what threatens them. Without doubt, these values are threatened in our society through that bourgeois individualism which certainly does not derive from the Christian idea of the individual person before God. Instead, our liberal-capitalistic economy of barter and competition has used this bourgeois individualism to conquer, not only the economic sector, but also the souls of people as well. The church's critique of the erosion of values in our society has to link up with a critique of social structures in society. Here also our churches could function as a pioneering force for social transformations which are not yet politically acceptable in our country. They would then be more successful than before in counteracting the impression that, in the political sector, the only kind of word they ever utter is directed to a backward looking stabilization without future perspectives.

In such a revolutionary move forward, two forces would ultimately meet together—the critique of society presented by the bishops, and the intentions of a basic-community church gradually developing among us.

Basic-Community Church within the Diagnosis of the World Church

1. My prognosis regarding the future of the church as basic community is accompanied and supported by a particular evaluation of

our "Catholic" situation as a universal church (and this situation is significantly broader and richer in tension than our Central European Christianities lead us to know). My assumption is that the churches of the third world will become, to an ever-increasing degree, a determining factor in the ecclesial situation of our own country. Therefore, we will no longer be able to understand and shape our own future as churches independently of the challenges and inspirations coming to us out of these poor churches. "Catholic" is no longer today simply a dogmatic attribute of our reality as a church—it is also an empirical attribute of this. Tactical provincialism is a luxury we can also do without as a church. If my view is correct, then the only dangerous "schism" threatening us today is the "separation" that would occur were we Christians of the first world to break apart the eucharistic table we share because we are unable to stand by the poor churches in their misery and oppression through a fundamental conversion, and because we refuse to listen to the prophecy of a common awakening which forces its way to us out of these poor churches.

I see, above all, three prophetic services which these poor churches can offer to our own church situation. First, they offer a way of being a person in solidarity which is not stamped by bourgeois individualism in our sense of the term, and yet at the same time which cannot simply be put in its place as belonging to a prebourgeois stage and therefore "needing development." A second gift is a new connection between salvation and liberation, between the experience of grace and of freedom, between mysticism and politics—as opposed to our prevailing separation of these realities, something motivated, not by the gospel but by what I have already called bourgeois unapproachability in regard to religion. The final service offered is that of a basic-community church, which we of course are not simply to copy, but which nevertheless contains inspirational power for our own church future. I know that people fear a new politicization of our church life if the basic-community church breaks in among us. But what have we really achieved with our "purely religious" parish communities? Quite apart from the fact that closer observation reveals their political neutrality to be only apparent anyway, are they really a place of the living experience of peace, a convivium of joy and consolation? Have they not become, in far too great a degree, organizations where contact among people is lost, where a dangerous alienation and a private isolation reign? If we really want to reanimate life within the church, don't we have a duty to establish church as basic community among us? Can the tensions arising from this be worse than the deadly indifference we experience all too frequently now?

2. Admittedly, a number of difficulties and obstacles stand in the way of forming a future basic-community church in our situation. These derive from our present pope, from our episcopal hierarchies, and lastly from a "progressive" bourgeois-liberal theology in our country. The common root of all their opposition to a basic-community church seems to me the ingrained Eurocentrism of their image of the church.

For reasons of brevity, I wish to mention only those barriers to the development of such a church among us which appear to be present in the attitude of the present pope. Overall, his pastoral priorities betray an energetic stabilization in a backwards direction. His aim is to restore a basic Eurocentric orientation within the discipline and praxis of the universal church. Despite, or perhaps because of, the pope's world travels, the intentions, inspirations, and promises represented by the poor churches of the third world are being increasingly removed from the agenda of the universal church. In contrast to certain tendencies under John XXIII and Paul VI, whereby these poor churches, with their prophecies and their historical mission, began to penetrate more and more into the center of our church, even to Rome, they are appearing once more as church dependencies.

In this connection, I want to make clear what my specific motives are in criticizing the pope. To take one example: I am not criticizing directly, as many of my colleagues do, the pope's refusal to allow birth control for the churches of these poor countries. In fact, I am not so certain about this question—particularly if one begins to look at the question of birth control for once through the eyes of the poor nations themselves, and not from the standpoint of the pharmaceutical companies. I am criticizing rather the threat posed by the pope to the emancipation of these churches in relation to the universal church. Another example: I would put hard questions regarding the obligatory celibacy enjoined once more by the pope on all priests. Yet I am not basing my position in this matter on the right to freedom and the basic human rights for all developed in the course of the bourgeois history of freedom. It is certainly possible to renounce such rights, whereas the same thing cannot be said for duties. I criticize the institution of obligatory celibacy because, in my opinion, it systematically prevents, among other things, the formation of future basic-community churches with a eucharistic center.

3. The reflections on the future of the church that I have put forward here for your consideration, reflect a basic experience which has been granted to me more and more frequently in recent times: this is the experience of a decisive change of awareness happening at the grass-roots level of our church. Often this new awareness does not go beyond a certain confusion and helplessness as to future strategy. It is frequently evidenced in the sensitivity of a bad conscience. I ask you with the deepest urgency: Do not be afraid of the powerlessness of this bad conscience of yours. It is with this experience, in fact, that many things begin to happen. And in this situation of far-reaching radical change, it is the courage to have a bad conscience, and the perseverance not to allow oneself to be talked out of it, that may be the only way today to have a conscience at all.

7.

Paradigm for a Political Culture of Peace

Ernesto Cardenal—A Productive Scandal

Do we know the kind of person we are honoring here today? Do we realize who it is who is being singled out by us now as a "Man of Peace"? Ernesto Cardenal, the poet, priest, and revolutionary from free Nicaragua, is a scandal. A singer of revolution as recipient of the Peace Prize? A poetry in which mysticism flows directly into politics and verse into revolutionary provocation as literature of peace? I quote from his "Epistle to Monsignor Casaldáliga":

> Recently a journalist asked me why I write poems:
>
> For the same reason as Amos, Nahum, Haggai and
> Jeremiah ....
> ....
> Now is not the time for literary criticism nor
> for surrealistic poems against military dictatorships.
> And why use metaphors when slavery is no
> metaphor
> and neither is death in the river of the dead
> nor the death squadron?
>
> Now the people are crying in pau-de-arara.
>
> Yet every cock which crows at night in Brasil
> is subversive now,
> it sings "Revoluçao."

. . . .
Monsignor, we are subversive,
a secret number on a card in God knows what
archive,
followers of the shabbily dressed proletarian and
visionary, of the
professional agitator, executed as an enemy of
the system.
As you know, for the subversive and the political
the cross was a torture, not a piece of jewelery
made from
rubies
on the breast of a bishop.

We are not allowed to read this text as exotic literature. Cardenal writes and makes poetry for us also. But in so doing he is and remains a scandal. That he can be understood and accepted as a "productive scandal" is the aim of the following reflections. These are concerned with:

—revolution and peace
—Cardenal and his country as a creative model for a new culture of peace
—the "new human being" of peace, in that country and in our own.

Revolution and Peace

In Germany we find it particularly difficult to bring the revolutionary act and the political attitude toward peace into harmony with each other. This difficulty is not by accident; its roots lie primarily in the political history of our country. Our historical and national identity is not founded upon a successful history of revolution. We are indeed a country of wars, but not of a successful revolution. Successful revolutions, if we want to use this term, took place at most in people's heads. In the practical realization of our freedom, however, we have remained till the present day those who live off foreign revolutions, especially the French Revolution. Subliminally, our political conscience is marked by a collective suspicion of every kind of revolution and its claim to create peace. The political fate of Nicaragua reminds us besides of our own most recent history, of our Somoza-like situation during Hitler's dictatorship. And this memory painfully airs a suspicion of guilt which continues to affect us like a collective trauma: the guilty suspicion namely that we for our part have exercised far too little resistance against our dictatorship, far less anyway than little Nicaragua against its own. This is another factor which makes an impartial evaluation of revolutionary resistance difficult for us. So much the more worthy of respect is it, then, when the Trade Association of the German Publishers bestows the Peace Prize on a writer like Ernesto Cardenal.

There exist, of course, other and more fundamental objections against uniting revolution and peace. As a theologian I would like to name one which affects the relationship of religion and revolution, mysticism and politics, and this is the protest of love against revolutionary violence. Can violence, which appears to be so profoundly contrary to love, serve in any way the creation of peace? This places Christians in a dilemma, and we can certainly begin with the assumption that Ernesto Cardenal experienced this conflict within himself as he went over—at a late hour—to the side of violent resistance. The Christian dilemma is rooted in the irrevocable unity of love of God and love of neighbor. Love of God can require the Christian to accept one's own powerlessness and suffer injustice toward oneself. With regard to love of neighbor, however, one is not permitted to come to terms with the powerlessness and oppression of others, of the "least of the brethren," nor to desire to love God, as it were, with one's back turned to these suffering people. In the language of the Sermon on the Mount, this means: the Christian is expected to turn the other cheek when he is struck on the right cheek, but he is not allowed to encourage someone else who is struck on the right cheek to turn the other cheek as well (cf. Mt. 5:39). For it is also true, and this is another demand of the Sermon on the Mount, that the Christian is not only responsible for what he does or fails to do, but also for what he allows to happen to others. Thus the Christian dilemma remains; outside the sphere of love it cannot be overcome nor can innocence be preserved, neither through a principle of unconditional nonviolence nor through a presumed neutrality, for the person who does not act and withholds his decision can share in the guilt for everything which is left undone, unattempted, and undelivered. And since nonviolence can also be disguised cowardice and can display the features of opportunism, the face of love is not marked by it unequivocally; love is able—for moments only and never as something sought after but always as something forced upon it—to take on the ominous face of violence as the expression of desperation. Yet this must happen in such a way that love always knows how much it is injured by every kind of violence. And I am confident that Ernesto Cardenal will one day speak also about these wounds of the revolution, wounds inflicted by the revolution upon itself.

Ernesto Cardenal: "The true revolutionary is an enemy of violence, he desires life and not death." There moves through Cardenal's whole work the utopia of a future society free of violence; everything in his work aims toward a violence-free culture of peace. Thus in his case revolutionary consciousness grows beyond the demonic cycle of violence.

Faced with the barbaric logic of violence, whereby violence continually gives rise to new violence, two kinds of reaction can be distinguished. One kind resigns itself to the logic of violence and puts forward this resignation as an anthropological condition: violence as the unavoidable expression of the human condition. The other starts out from the principle that it is certainly worthwhile to struggle for a political life which is free from violence, though not free from conflict and contradiction, presupposing one knows that the goal of nonviolence aspired to is never placed *above* the means which are used to achieve it, but rather that it must emerge *from* these means themselves. The cultural level of a politics can be deciphered not only from the elevated goals it proclaims, but above all from the means it employs. In this sense, Cardenal's political and poetic struggle aims at the *transformation of political means,* so that from these violence-free means goals of peace, goals of nonviolent life may at last emerge. His look is not one of violence, but of love. He has eyes for the victims—for the weeping mothers and the wasted children in his exploited people, as well as for the anonymous structures of violence in which a dependence of the third world on the first, a dependence disguised as "development," continues to operate. But he has eyes for the victims within our consumerist-capitalist world also: we might recall, for example, his poem about Marilyn Monroe.

Cardenal's political poetry seeks not only to unmask, not even exclusively to accuse, above all it seeks to *save*. Its basic stance is not aggression, but rather "protection": it seeks to protect, to rediscover that which as victim of our domineering civilization has long been forgotten or repressed; whatever in the conversation of the victors (which often advances itself as the language of God) has long since become speechless and dumb. It attempts to recall not only what has succeeded but also what has been ruined, not only the realized but also the lost, and attempts thus to direct itself against the monotonous victoriousness of reality as it has come to be. This is the impetus, for example, behind Cardenal's inclination toward the Native American, pre-Hispanic poetry and culture of Latin America, given explicit expression in his epic "For the Indians of America." He is not copying some kind of primitive language pattern from them, in order to flirt with it in the world of our exhausted poetry. No, he is continuing to speak their interrupted history, the peace dialogue of the Indian people with nature which we have disrupted; he continues this dialogue imperceptibly into our own language, in order to break the latter's objective activity of violence through the power of his poetry. His poetic struggle is directed against a civilization in which human beings have built their identity upon the subjugation of nature, and then transferred this principle of subjugation into the realm of interpersonal and social relationships. Such a poetic criticism of our domineering virtues is not the least significant contribution of Cardenal to a critique of violence and to the construction of a culture of peace. To achieve this, he has learned not only from Marx and his revolutionary pathos but also from Gandhi's ethic of nonviolence, not only from the wrath of the biblical prophets but also from the gentleness of the Indios.

Creative Model of a Culture of Peace

A revolution can always be evaluated, among other things, by the faces which emerge from within it. In Nicaragua the faces were not of generals, functionaries, and bureaucrats, but of poets, priests, and teachers. Cynics of power will contemptuously set aside so admittedly fragile an alliance between culture and politics. Others will allow it to exist as a typically "developmental" manifestation of politics in an "underdeveloped" country, yet of course without signifying any impulse to change for the highly complex societies of our first world with their specific divisions of labor. I wish nevertheless to put forward the expectation that in Nicaragua a new relationship is being sketched between culture and political society, a project for a societal formation of identity which contains within itself provocative or exemplary force for a political culture of peace everywhere.

It seems important to me to situate and appreciate Ernesto Cardenal within this politico-cultural process. Only thus will we avoid misunderstanding or underestimating his work which continually injures and breaks through conventional poetic patterns. In him there finds expression *the project of a basic-community culture* in which, through the primary means of language, people are to attain religious and sociopolitical identity.

If we see Cardenal in this way, we will certainly not underestimate his *Psalms* which are read today throughout the world. In these psalms, Cardenal speaks in fact a language of prayer which has authentically taken up into itself society's conflicts and sufferings: this language brings out clearly how much humanity would lose of its potential for expressing crises and suffering in language, were the centuries-old language of prayers to disappear from its midst. Admittedly, the poet speaks here as "representative" for the suffering, the oppressed, and the persecuted. They themselves remain speechless, the mortal threat to their identity is denounced but not, as yet, overcome in language. This changes in another book which has also been widely disseminated since then, *The Gospel in Solentiname,* the transcripts of dialogues on individual passages of the Gospels which Cardenal conducted on the island of Solentiname in the Great Sea of Nicaragua with "his" poor, landless peasants during the common Sunday liturgies. Here he is no longer just the poet with compassionate thoughts and meditations; instead he takes on Socrates' maieutic role of guiding, helping, listening, and undergoing a painful learning process himself as he speaks with the oppressed a language of suffering and hope. In this case, he becomes the inspirer and witness of a grass-roots culture in which human beings confronting the deepest humiliation and threat attain the initial perspectives for a new identity in solidarity.

This formation of identity takes place through *the gospel*. Not the gospel that has been stripped of its images and demythologized to suit the allegedly unsurpassable truisms of modern society. Their gospel is being taken instead in a shockingly literal fashion, is being heard and gropingly understood by people who refuse simply to adapt the gospel to their own miserable situation; instead they set out under the exhortation of the gospel so to change their situation that this situation itself might better fit the spirit and the prophecy of such a gospel. And in this fashion, their Christian identity which has been awakened and formed through the gospel has made them at the same time subjects of their political liberation. Religious and politico-cultural identity formation go hand in hand here, in contrast to our European cultural history in which the processes of the Enlightenment and of political freedom have always led more in the direction of a mass weakening of religious identity.

Free Nicaragua is seeking today to practice this basic-community culture in the shape of a societal process of learning which has become known under the slogan of "alphabetization." This does not involve the unemancipated being trained by the emancipated and the knowledgeable in the proper functioning of a societal system: instead, through a total social process of reciprocal learning and instruction, a new societal consciousness and a new collective identity are to emerge for the first time. A people that was previously rendered voiceless by oppression and powerlessness is not only learning, it is also teaching, instructing the teachers about its own history of suffering, and binding them to its own historical memory. This kind of grass-roots enlightenment is precisely what prevents a politically liberated people from becoming potentially the manipulatable masses of a self-appointed revolutionary elite. A people experiences itself as *subject* of the new societal process and does not allow itself, under the influence of propagandist persuasion, to relinquish its own memory and the symbols of a longed-for identity preserved within this memory.

This new societal learning, this kind of "people's culture" involving a basic-community enlightenment in the service of the formation of identity is as foreign to our Western civilizations as it is to Eastern socialist societies. Would there not be a possible invitation in this for us, not just to admire what they are doing but also to use our own creativity to do the same, or something similar, ourselves? I know that this kind of question exposes me at once to the charge of naiveté. How could our highly developed and highly complex society possibly find in Cardenal's Nicaragua a model for a political culture of peace? Yet what does "development" mean? If we measure it by economic growth and the gross national product, then we are certainly highly developed. But if we take as our standard of "development" the power enabling us to form identity, then Nicaragua, which is economically not only our weakly developed partner but also our victim, could be our cultural exemplar.

We ourselves are confronted by the task of shaping a new identity. Such a task is, in my eyes, *the* decisive politico-cultural work of peace which is today demanded of us, the citizens of the first world. One of the epochal characteristics of our situation is the inescapable and irrevocable entry of the third world into our own socio-economic and political situation. This fact is the point of departure for any shaping of peace today. It precludes in fact every form of tactical provincialism in our politics and also every form of ingrained Eurocentrism in our political view of the world. I am referring to the kind of attitude that hopes to bridge the opposition between the poor countries of the third world and the rich ones of the first world with a concept of smoothly flowing development which remains always under our control—an attitude which excludes decisive changes being demanded of us ourselves. People who thus define victims as weakly developed partners are making apathy the foundation of their political culture. But such a thing would in the end lead only to self-assertion devoid of reflection and vision; it would not lead to the political and moral shaping of peace. This shaping of peace does, in fact, demand from us in our situation a new societal way of forming identity: We can no longer define our own social and political identity apart from or over against the poverty, misery, and oppression in the third world. This new identity is not yet politically acceptable. It is the task of a political culture of peace.

The patterns for forming identity already available to us in our political cultural history are inadequate to this task. Bourgeois individualism, as it has emerged from the Reformation, the Enlightenment, and the French Revolution, together with the economic structures connected with them, has propelled the idea of the individual in so abstract and isolated a fashion that the bourgeois individuality that has been formed by this historically is today capable of only a feeble kind of solidarity. But it would need a truly strong capacity for solidarity if, in the process of building this new societal identity, we are to save the unrelinquishable achievements of our bourgeois history of freedom and of Enlightenment, and if we are to avert the barbarism of a political negation of the individual. The European Enlightenment has remained to this very day too dualistic; it still keeps on reproducing the opposition between cultural elites and culturally isolated masses, between a kind of culture of experts and a culturally deprived grass-roots level. I remind you simply of the culture catastrophe in the Nazi period. Why in fact did the German people not fight back more effectively when the Nazis in the cultural terror robbed them of their best art and literature and desecrated these? Was it only because of opportunism and political cowardice, because ''the people'' were so much more cowardly than the persecuted cultural figures themselves? Or was the reason rather that ''the people'' were unable to recognize sufficiently these cultural works as their own?

I am therefore taking the risk of speaking of our own need for a political basic-community culture also (whereby I give preference to the word ''basic community'' because there are historical and sociological grounds which prevent us, in Germany, from unhesitatingly using the word ''people'' [*Volk*] in this context). This grass-roots or basic-community culture would have to overcome at last that ''truncated Enlightenment'' among us by which the propertied citizen became too exclusively the bearer of political culture, depriving other groups and classes of cultural power or rendering them totally invisible.

The *beginnings* of such a basic-community culture are certainly already present among us. I restrict myself to an example from the cultural area which is most familiar to me, the area of religion and church. Impelled precisely by the realization that the poor churches of the third world are not just cases calling for the solicitude of the rich churches in this country, but instead that our very identity as Christians is involved in responding to the religio-political prophecy of these churches, there is cautiously developing among us something like a basic-community religion, a kind of basic-community church in distinction to the purely paternalistic church taking care of people and also to the bourgeois services church. Such a basic-community church is also, in comparison with these other models, much more politically conscious and differentiated—yet not in the sense in which a basic-community culture is typically accused of a bad politicization of culture; it is not submitting itself compliantly to a preconceived politics which has already been established somewhere else; it is much rather involved in the generation of a new political consciousness, so that the new way of forming identity which is inexorably demanded of us might at last become politically acceptable in a democratic sense.

I do not hesitate to describe this process of creating a political basic-community culture as our own form of an ongoing literacy campaign, or of *post-alphabetization*. This can find in Cardenal's Nicaragua, if not an immediate model, then at least a powerful impetus. The power of a political culture always manifests itself in its relative capacity to develop itself in the encounter with other political cultures.

The "New Human Being" of Peace, There and Here

In a talk with Hermann Schulz, his publisher in Wuppertal, who has done more than anyone else to make the poet and his country a living presence among us, Cardenal spoke, provocatively enough, of the "holiness of the revolution." Before we protest or make distinctions, we should perhaps think of all those things which we, for our part, have worldlessly proclaimed as holy, everything that has long since become a secular myth for us: our bourgeois unapproachability; the myth of our Central European logic of development, according to which we ourselves always represent the peak of societal evolution; the myth of the unchangeableness of bourgeois society, to which all is subject and which permeates everything, including religion, turning this in the meantime into bourgeois religion, the political religion of the bourgeois in which our society establishes itself once more and in which God can indeed still be quoted but scarcely appears as worthy of adoration, since God does not break in, cast down or raise up, but instead over-arches, as a "value," our preconceived bourgeois identity. At the same time, I do not wish to take over Cardenal's expression. I would prefer to speak of *the loneliness and the vulnerability of this revolution* and of the "new human being" of peace being sought and celebrated within it. The stability of this peace project contains in the end its own still precarious preconditions.

On the one hand, it depends, as everything I said previously shows, on the successful realization of a culture of peace *among ourselves*. This "new human being" of peace must come into being among us as well; a new societal principle of individuation has to break through in our midst also, one that leads neither to bourgeois individualism nor to a collectivism which negates indi-viduality, but rather to a new solidarity in which we of the first world no longer achieve our social and political identity *against* others, against people of weaker countries and classes, but instead *together with* them. This "conversion to peace" (known in the Scriptures as the "conversion of hearts" and not limited to a change of attitude alone, since a change of attitude alone does not change an attitude at all)—this "conversion to peace" would be our fundamental contribution to Nicaragua's project of peace.

There exist also, of course, internal preconditions for an endur-ing unfolding of a revolutionary culture of peace *over there*. Er-nesto Cardenal can speak about these much better than I. I would like, nevertheless, to be allowed to make reference to these by way of conclusion, and I do this more in the form of a request and an expectation. "Forgiving," as Tomás Borge, the country's Interior Minister who was himself severely tortured during the revolution-ary resistance, put it to me, "is for us a revolutionary virtue." And free Nicaragua has taken this seriously, has abrogated the death penalty, and has sought not to liquidate the former enemies of the revolution but instead to use all their powers and opportunities to resocialize them. To be sure, forgiving is only really possible to those who also hold themselves capable of guilt. And thus it will be important for all that the "new human being" of peace in Nic-aragua considers himself also to be capable of guilt, and does this precisely in the name of his revolutionary conscience! For to be capable of guilt is not, in fact, a sign of impotence and oppression but is instead one of the great demands placed upon human freedom.

At some point the first enthusiasm over the success of the revolution will fade and the quasi-messianic glory around the new country will darken. When that time comes, this moral evaluation of the revolution, this readiness on the part of revolutionary life to accept its own capacity for guilt, can preserve free Nicaragua from simply projecting outwards the conflicts and contradictions emerging within it, preserve it also from reinforcing its newly won identity at the root by means of new compulsions to make enemies. I know how great such a demand is, but the hope is also great which is tied to this country.

Dear Ernesto, I have experienced the will to such a shaping of peace in you, among your co-workers in the political struggle, among the people of your country. I know that, as a victor, you will not forget what you have said as one persecuted about the exercise of power, about purges and violence. And you will also have, should it be needed, that other revolutionary courage, not only the initial courage to begin a revolutionary resistance against oppression and exploitation, but also the further courage to resist everything which threatens to betray and weaken the ideals of this revolution. All that makes your revolution so vulnerable in this quarrelsome and violence-filled world, yet by that very fact so full of promise also. It becomes thereby an experiment in a new culture of peace, cunningly introduced behind the back of world politics. If it were to fail, in one way or another, we would all be one hope of peace poorer. In the service of this hope is your work, your poetic and political struggle for Nicaragua—and for us. *"Nicara-* science at all.

For Further Reading

Cardenal, Ernesto. *The Gospel in Solentiname*. 3 vols. Orbis, 1976, 1978, 1979.
———, *Psalms*. Crossroad, 1981.
———, *Love*. Crossroad, 1981.
Freire, Paulo. *Pedagogy of the Oppressed*. Continuum, 1970.

8.

The Faith of the Reformers

*The following address was given in 1968. It was published after-
ward in the weekly newspaper* Publik *(see "List of Sources") with
the following note attached: "This article is the transcript of an
improvised lecture given on December 5, a lecture to which the
author felt himself impelled above all by an item in the previous
day's press. According to this news item, it should not be long
until, in Rome, 'Ratzinger, Rahner and Metz would be denounced'
also."*

*Although this talk was given a long time ago, I have included it
here since, unfortunately, it remains still acutely relevant. Another
reason is that this talk may indicate the basic pathos out of which
my suggestions and my criticisms regarding the postconciliar
church emerge, even if the theological-political viewpoint has
shifted in the most recent talks, and the perspectives—we may
hope—have thereby become more precisely articulated.*

The problems of the Second Vatican Council are certainly not
identical with the problems of the postconciliar church. However,
in my opinion, this makes it all the more important that the specific
character of the Council as model for us should be taken seriously
and put into practice. This refers to what has often been called the
"spirit" of the Council—which ought not to be suspected of being
simply a spirit of cheap adaptation and modish innovation, but must
be recognized as a spirit of freedom and of the courage that empowers us to critical self-reflection.

It is strange that all those who like to invoke the spirit against

107

the "innovators" do not shrink from asserting that this spirit was not really present at the last Council. This spirit of the Council—a troubled expression that you yourselves may often hear and one to which I am committed—seems in truth to be endangered.

Groups are evidently already mobilizing again within the church who distrust the Council and want to drive out its spirit from among us. Veiled and extremely subtle forms of mutual inquisition are already emerging again, and the fact that this inquisition is masked does not make it more harmless, but rather much more questionable. Is there not an obvious danger that the reforms aimed at by the Council will be stopped before they have really begun? And that we are fearfully settling down again before we have risked the great, liberating leap forward? A drastic image for our situation might be this: I have often had the fear that everything to do with renewal in the church resembles the June bug, which begins pumping and pumping its wings for its first flight, but before it takes off, others come alone and say: "For God's sake, you know you won't fly, flying is far too dangerous!" Or it is like the situation of the child who never learns to walk because he is naturally afraid of falling and because there are many people around who know that walking includes falling. In fact, the upright position is difficult to learn and cannot in the end be acquired without occasional falls. Yet such a position is a sign of that freedom invoked at the Council, and upon which the chance of renewal depends. One should not persuade a child *not* to try to walk on the grounds that it is far too dangerous. One should not seek to undertake a Counter Reformation before the reform has really begun, nor should one talk the whole time about chaos and unrest. This situation should not become a signal for calling everything off and putting things back where they were, just for the reasons that the reality is becoming more complex to grasp and more difficult to deal with, that responsibilities are being divided, and that we have finally to begin trusting the initiative of the spirit more.

Does this not show with painful clarity that there exists in the church something like a constitutional mistrust of the freedom of the spirit, of that freedom which is nevertheless bestowed upon us as a gift in the liberating message of Jesus, and that obviously belongs to the "freedom of the children of God" which Paul emphatically proclaimed? Is it not indeed precisely that reign of God, attested to and promised in the gospel, which liberates us for such freedom? And only in this kind of freedom, not without it or against it, does God want to rule, provided we do not seek to misunderstand the proclamation of God's power and reign as a religious ideology of domination.

However, freedom cannot be simulated in the long run, so this will be the decisive test of what will happen to the Council in the postconciliar church. We hear language about reforms, yet in most cases lacking any real desire to experience painful changes. Such changes would really have to affect everyone, not just particular small groups. All must be affected throughout the church, from top to bottom. And yet the call for this reform will not become silent. It simply cannot be neutralized ever again.

There are certain things which, once they have been called in doubt, cannot be rescued. And sometimes when I look at the situation of the church and especially church authority, it reminds me of the case of the emperor in the fairy tale, *The Emperor's New Clothes,* where the child has torn apart the overall context of delusion with his spontaneous shout of "Look, that man's got nothing on!" This kind of critique cannot be ignored, nor treated as if it never happened; from now on it has to be reckoned with. And the church can no longer return to its former "peace and order" but must learn to live with this rebellion and with the objections of critical freedom, assimilating them in a vital way into its own life. Absolute monarchy, so it seems to me, was already dead the moment it was first called in doubt, for it had no possibility of assuming this doubt—as freedom—into itself and of assimilating it politically. A question reaching to the very roots of the church involves its readiness to live with the conflicts of critical freedom and to grasp these as an intrinsic element of its own being—as well as the measure of its success in so doing.

This is not only postulated for an elitist and superrefined minority of intellectuals in the church; it seems instead to be emerging increasingly as a vital question for the church precisely as a people's church. For the problem of tomorrow's church will certainly not be primarily the critical intellectuals, but much more the ordinary people, the much quoted "flock of Christ," which today itself appears profoundly disturbed—not by a critical theology but by the institution of the church itself. It is, in truth, the actual fact of the church's changing that has generated confusion and an identity crisis among these people. The church has, in fact, really changed in many areas, at least since the last Council. And there is no way this can be altered, for if the attempt were made to reverse this change, the confusion would only be greater and an even more oppressive impression of arbitrariness would be given: the impression that the church itself no longer knows whether it is on its head or its feet.

The frequently invoked confusion among the faithful is certainly not produced primarily by a critical theology; its real cause is the fact that the church has exposed the faithful in a hardhearted way to change, without having opened to them a critical understanding of the church's own need to be reformed. "Deeds left undone often unleash a catastrophic lack of consequences" (Stanislaw Lem). How should the simple faithful keep on understanding the church in all its changes? How should they not feel duped when they have no critical understanding of their church, no mature relationship to it: this being the only way to see continuity in change or to know that it is exactly this change which belongs to the historical identity of an *ecclesia semper reformanda?* It is not an excess of criticism but a catastrophic lack of fundamental and practiced critical freedom in the church which is one of the causes of our present crisis. And this lack is making the flock of Christ into the central focus of crisis in the church of tomorrow. Let no one underestimate the religious identity crisis of our devout parents! Who will rescue them in the end from a terrible indifferentism, from an antichurch cynicism or a sceptical resignation, through which an ever widening and fatal wasteland is being created between the church as institution and the faithful?

Someone, therefore, who insists on the development of critical freedom in the church and pursues the dissemination of this freedom within the church's consciousness, thereby correcting the purely authoritarian way the faithful expect knowledge to be given them by the institutional church—such a person is not working toward the destruction of the church, nor is he acting in any kind of hardhearted way toward the ordinary church people. What this represents, instead, is a struggle for the future prospects of a committed church membership of tomorrow. On the other hand, a person who sees in the development of this critical consciousness a symptom of defection must ask himself whether he really wants the church of Jesus Christ and not, instead, some kind of religious sectarianism devoid of critical sense and without humor. He may be confusing church spirituality with a form of blind voluntarism.

It is not a question of reassembling allegedly broken structures: the real issue is of living in the church, at last, with this critical intention, with this freedom. That is important and must be made public; above all, it needs to be said by those who, in fact, are there to teach theology. The present situation is strange, and yet it is also typical, for there are many such examples in church history: examples of making the reformers ineffective or neutralizing them by casting suspicion on their faith or by allowing them a certain fool's freedom (although this figure should cause us to reflect since Herod himself, after all, attempted to dispose of Jesus' claim by making him into a fool!).

All too quickly the critical will to reform is distrusted as being liberal minimalism. All too quickly the faith of the reformers is being doubted, and the rebellion of critical freedom in the church is being assailed as the apotheosis of unfaith. All too quickly the impression is being created that the reforms are designed to make things easier for us in regard to faith and not more difficult. Such an insinuation is, of course, disastrous and ultimately fatal for any reform which is meant to be substantial and derived from faith. This must, therefore, be changed. It must be made clear that these reforms emerge, through a painful and critical process, from faith itself; that it is not liberal minimalism and a modernistic desire for adaptation which are attacking everything, but the passionate restlessness of faith itself. In consequence, the struggle here is not for modernity or nonmodernity, but rather for the future outlook of faith.

It follows that the reformers must themselves have the courage to turn around this reproach of having insufficient faith, or faintheartedness, or just pretended faith. They have to challenge the good will and the good conscience of those who think the very fact that they never change a thing automatically makes them more "committed" to the church. They ought not to be allowed to operate with the distinction that "objectively much of what they do is false, but subjectively they have good will." For then it would be finally clear that the issue is not the profound faith of those hostile to reform over against the faintheartedness and modernistic desire for adaptation of the reformers. The suspicion must be expressed that it may be the other way round. The issue is a question of faith, on the one side and on the other; and every reform that seeks the possibility of growth must extricate itself from this kind of dilemma. Or are we to reinforce the fatal impression that reactionary mentalities enjoy a privileged domicile in the church? That Christian faith could in any case have less difficulty and fewer problems in union with that kind of mentality rather than with the restlessness of reformist attitudes?

It is true that every situation has its fellow travellers and opportunists; and so fellow travellers and opportunists are present in the reform also. It may also include critical cynics (sometimes created when the thin-skinned or the irritable are pushed beyond their limits and lack that reformer's "elephant hide" which can still cope with yet another disappointment). Yet which of us is allowed to judge the reformist awakening from this point of view? What is really at stake in such a reform is uniquely the issue of faith and its unity in truth, and accompanying this, of course, change in the structures of the church. For a "pure" change of opinions does not ultimately change opinions at all. In addition, there are forms and structures of church life which seem like coagulated mistakes, like ecclesial sins in a fixed state of accumulation. In this case, the loyalty of the church toward itself cannot and should not degenerate into a persistence in such mistakes.

In such a situation, a critical theology also cannot and should not seek to "understand" too much and "interpret" too much; it must contradict decisively, for the very interpreting of such mistakes is also a disguised form of persisting in them. A theology of this kind, which understands itself as a theology of the church despite the fact, or rather precisely because of the fact, that it does not betray or render ineffective its critical freedom in this same church, is always more dangerous for the church itself than a liberal theology which seeks more or less to ignore the fate of the concrete church. This theology is, naturally, also more dangerous than any integralist theology of reconciliation that avoids the risk of critically taking sides and does not liberate but simply justifies (in a subtle way) what is already there.

Concrete tendencies are certainly present in the church which give the impression of a purely liberalist minimalizing. That is, of course, no reform at all. But closer inspection makes one ask if the only cause of this is such a liberalizing tendency, and nothing else, or whether we simply do not have enough creative phantasy in the church to counteract this tendency with something else, something much more serious and profound.

The reform is not concerned with making it easier for us in regard to faith. In the future the reformers themselves will have to find a form of argument that is not so hypersensitive. We would really need a new Kierkegaard, a new Pascal, Newman or St. Francis. Yet such exemplary figures alone would not help us in our condition; the issue is no longer whether this person or another should come forward in an elite kind of way as critic of the church and as reformer. Today the reform must encompass everyone, or else it will not succeed. And yet as regards these kinds of model leaders who would manifest the meaning of reform, my feeling is that we are so poor in the church today that we not only do not have such figures, but in addition we do not even know what they should look like.

I ask firstly: In the present institutional attitude of the church, is there not too little trust in the power of the Spirit? Consider the fearful reactions in the present situation. What is happening there? I am really afraid that today the church as institution reacts and behaves in virtually the same pattern by which all institutions seek to preserve themselves and to survive. This resemblance is all too evident to me, so much so that after being continually asked what is specifically Christian in my theology, I want to ask in return: What is specifically Christian about the behavior of the institution? Is it really evident in the image the church manifests of itself that it is not an end in itself; that its purpose is to "unmake" itself, in the literal and dialectical sense of the term, on behalf of the reign of God? And that by this very fact the church would have to differ from all other institutions with their laws of self-preservation and survival?

I ask secondly: Why, then, do the reformers always let themselves be driven so quickly into the corner with the reproach "Will you also go?" They really ought not to let this language about the "little flock" serve as a self-justification for a church that does not want to walk the painful path of renewal, a church that adamantly refuses to journey into the open frontier of as yet untested ways of living. The expression, the "little flock," can undoubtedly be understood in a sense favorable to the reformers also. In any case, it ought not to justify a kind of attitude which refuses any longer to confront the challenges of the world around it. For the church is not, primarily, "small" by representing a small, specially selected group, but rather by making itself "small" in the fluctuation of its struggle with the world. Nor can the church itself choose the cross of its poverty and its smallness, for it is said of this very cross that it in no way stands in the Holy of Holies but "outside." Crucifixion never occurs in the Holy Place, but always "outside the gates of the city." It is there that we experience the insignificance and the poverty of the cross, which we cannot get rid of or choose of our own will. But where is the greater readiness to take up this same cross? In the will to undergo painful transformations of our own familiar ways of life in the church because we are faced with the challenges of our world? Or in the questionable self-certainty of so many enemies of reform? On which side do we find the passionate readiness to face up to the "scandal of Christianity"? There, where the only place people are looking is inside themselves? Not in my view. The issue is not liberalizing and adaptation, but the very question we are discussing.

I ask thirdly: A question for the theologians themselves: Do we not often lack what I want to call here a "second courage"? This second courage is something like the ethos of a theological discovery of truth, whereby truth itself appears as a theory-praxis problem, and our wrestling with the ecclesial-social consequences of new theological insights therefore belongs to the truth of these insights themselves. Authentic theological renewal, in fact, never takes place only in the heads of theologians. It may begin there, with the "first courage" to nonconformity, the courage to break through the established canon of prejudices, to swim against the stream, to risk losing the good will of church officials and former friends. It may begin with the almost childlike courage to seek a new immediacy, a new critical spontaneity which sees through and breaks open a totally dominant complex of mystification.

All that is important and certainly cannot be attained without a fundamental effort of the spirit. Yet the theological will to reform should not end there. For this new truth, which is at issue in the theological awakening, is not an idealist property present within the esoteric community of the few who have the knowledge. This truth is present where it becomes the truthfulness of the church and the credibility of the faithful themselves; in short, where it attains its social basis in the transformed praxis of the community of believers. But this is the very reason why, in my view, all theological reformers have need of a second courage. I find this second courage often lacking, above all, among progressive and reformist theologians; that is, among those who have definitely evidenced the first courage, those who were able to bring their critical and liberating theological insights to successful account at the last Council. They appear not infrequently to be now retreating again, just when the positions they stand for threaten to become public, common property, indeed to become popular. What is behind this attitude? Is it fear of the consequences of one's own theology? A covert idealist or gnostic prejudice whereby the truth can, after all, only be with the few? Or a dangerous confusion between the elitist and the committed attitude? Or, finally, a fatal reversal of one principle—that truth is never legitimized through majorities—into another principle—that truth cannot and should not be with the majority, which means never with the public opinion of the church as a people? Perhaps we are dealing with a covert, unavowed disdain of the church as a people? A last mistrust of their maturity?

Whatever the reasons may be, everything now depends in this situation on the reformers showing the second courage I have described; the courage to persevere where their cause—at last!—is beginning to become the cause of the church precisely as a people. The second courage, which involves solidarity, continuing the initial courage, which involved nonconformity. This is the courage to let oneself be disparaged in the church as "modish" and still to remain "progressive" now that the church is beginning, from below to become "progressive" in a process which is gradual and certainly not without error. Only in this way will the promises of the Council be fulfilled. Only thus will the reformist renewal of the church itself achieve victory. And this victory will be a victory of ecumenism, which can only advance by paying the high price of church reform. And this price must be paid by all, out of everyone's pocket, from the pope to the very last believer, as well as by the theologians with the second courage of reformers. For if this renewal is to come true, it must give to the community of believers themselves a new countenance.

I ask fourthly: Do those people have a greater faith in the spirit of the church who want to lock the church away, as it were, from what is called "the world"? For we know that it is precisely the specific nature of the church not to be able to live from its own resources; it is never allowed, in fact, to direct its gaze only within. That would be heresy. Its founding began in that process whereby the synagogue ceased to live from its own familiar traditions and went forth out of its own land and its own language into the turbulence of a world, into the diaspora of those very people who shared this awakening. Thus began the founding of the church: with the realization that faith and church can only live where they do not want to live simply by reproducing pregiven religious traditions.

This church belongs to the Son and becomes his church only when it goes beyond itself, when it risks going out into the unknown, about which the Son himself said that this unknown was his own possession. This question of openness or of moving outward, which is once more being looked on with amusement or is suspected of masking only liberalism and a cowardly faith, is not dealing with adaptation or what is fashionably topical. On the contrary, it is concerned with the church's identity. The church would cease to be itself if it no longer sought this unknown as Christ's own possession, if it no longer sought for and discovered something there which it does not have of itself. The church would become heretical if it believed it could understand itself and its mission only out of its own reality.

It is therefore unacceptable that only those are held to be believers who gather, in pre-Pentecost fashion, behind closed doors and drawn curtains, then, if possible, go out to snare others in inquisitorial dialogue, as we hear in the Scriptures: *"ut caperent Jesum in sermone"* (but in regard to the Pharisees, not to Jesus' disciples!).

It is unacceptable that those who risk going out into this unknown in order not to break the bent reed nor put out the smouldering wick, in fact to light this again and again, are being presented as minimalists and pure humanists.

It is unacceptable that the only people counted as believers are those who cover over all unrest, the way fire is covered over in the stove.

It is unacceptable that people should be considered, from the very outset, to be weak and vulnerable in their faith simply because they know themselves to be really troubled and feel themselves responsible for all those who now stand apart in attitudes of protest or cynicism or indifference. Such people are dismayed that the enthusiasm of young people today can no longer be ignited for a message proclaimed by the church.

What, then, must have happened to this message? Here I can only plead for decisiveness—for decisiveness and passion. Nor are we really helped much by mere mediation, by a generalized "both-and"; "try this thing—try the other thing; the truth lies in the middle." Yes, it does lie, in the middle—*buried!*

Epilogue
On My Own Behalf

1. The first chapter in this volume, "Messianic or Bourgeois Religion," which comprises the address I gave at the 1978 Freiburg Catholic Congress, was sharply criticized by the president of the German Bishops' Conference, Cardinal Höffner, in his opening report to the autumn plenary session of the 1979 German Bishops' Conference in Fulda.[1] Since many thousands of copies of this report were distributed by the Office of the German Bishops' Conference, I cannot pass over this criticism in silence. In all honesty, I am unable to see how my Freiburg address, if taken in its total thrust and in all its details, could become for Cardinal Höffner a paradigm of the "false path of minimalism."[2] Certainly, no one in Freiburg itself understood it in this sense, least of all the bishop debating with me. In fact, I had to reckon much more with the opposite objection.

What is then "minimalist" about a talk which explicitly and throughout is guided by the supposition that "the reason for the church's loss of appeal is not that it demands too much from people, but that it offers, in fact, too little challenge or else does not present its demands clearly enough as priorities of the gospel itself"? Since this talk was precisely about the recovery of a Christianity of discipleship in opposition to a superstructure Christianity in the style of bourgeois religion, with what right can it be denounced as a sell-out of Christianity, against which we have to reclaim the seriousness of Christian discipleship and the love of the cross? And how should it be "minimalist," once the total thrust of

119

my address is seen, when my starting point is that we will overcome the present pastoral crisis of church life less through "legal
rigorism" than through the practice of "evangelical radicalism"?
And what would be "minimalist" about the question "whether
such legal rigorism is the way both to overcome the contradictions
of bourgeois religion in Christianity and to make the Christian alternatives to a bourgeois way of life really visible? Or, put in
another way, whether this is the direction needed to heal the split
between the messianic virtues of the gospel we preach and those
the bourgeois practice, that is, whether conversion leading to discipleship will become possible"?

What, finally, is "minimalist" about my position that the rigorous refusal to administer sacraments to those who have failed in
their marriages should not dispense the church from its "real" pastoral task of uncovering and attacking the societal roots of this failure: namely, the insidious spread of the bourgeois principle of exchange beyond the economic sector into the psychic foundations of
social life together, so that interpersonal relationships are increasingly subjected to the anonymous pressure of interchangeability and
transitoriness? The extent to which my critical view of obligatory
priestly celibacy—as "cloaking over a Christendom which has totally lost its radical character"—does not aim simply at an agree-
able bourgeois form of existence; in fact the extent to which this
kind of imputation contradicts the total intention of my statement
can effortlessly be gathered from the text by any impartial reader.

I do not see the critical freedom of theology in the church as
being directed against the unity of the church. This can already be
gathered from that early text of mine, printed in this volume, on
"The Faith of the Reformers." Yet how should I, in my own turn,
react to a criticism like Cardinal Höffner's? Can I interpret it other
than as a tactical misunderstanding—perhaps according to the de-
vice that something *cannot* exist if it *should not* exist? Is the pastoral crisis of our church life so much under control, then, that
every new perspective which cannot be accommodated within the
prevailing categories is to be rejected from the outset and hastily
branded as a "false path"? Which of us is really levelling down in
this case? And which of us is effectively contributing here to the
deepening of the schism between church and life? Which of us,

finally, is aggravating the climate of mistrust between magisterium and theology, a problem which is deplored time and again precisely by the bishops themselves? I am not asking this question in order to vent my aggression. It emerges rather out of a sense of grief and a certain perplexity.

Or would I have been better advised to keep silent with my critique of the West German church as an institution of bourgeois religion, because "in Metz's system of 'bourgeois religion' the theology professor as a well-paid state official would indeed [have to] be included also, something Metz leaves out"?[3] I am certainly aware, together with quite a few of my colleagues, of the dilemma of a bourgeois professor of theology, the state official who trains people in discipleship. I do not conceal this from my students, nor in the publicized account I have given as to why I am a Christian.[4] Does this rob me of every moral competence for criticizing Christianity as bourgeois religion? How can the individual act here other than in a divided state, as some kind of "traitor"? If we are ever to emerge from these contradictions, we can do so only together with each other. And we must escape from this babylonian captivity of bourgeois religion! In Freiburg I was openly asked about my salary and how I intended to use it in the light of my talk. I tried to answer such questions honestly. Since then such inquiries are addressed to me more and more frequently. Is a theology which provokes and attracts such questions false or deceitful?

2. In the summer of 1979 it became public that my appointment from Münster to the University of Munich—to take over the chair for Fundamental Theology there, which also included looking after an Ecumenical Institute—was blocked by an intervention of Cardinal Ratzinger. This event provoked widespread and persistent public attention. As the person immediately concerned, I deemed it neither meaningful nor required of me to intervene in the public discussion. So much the more grateful was I that Karl Rahner, in a comprehensive statement which received attention far beyond the frontiers of our country, protested against Cardinal Ratzinger's method of behavior and that of the Bavarian Minister of Education responsible for the matter.[5] In this protest of Rahner everything, in fact, seems to me to be said which needed saying about this

"case." Meanwhile Cardinal Ratzinger has published a reply to Rahner's protest.[6] I am unable to accept his claim to have furthered, by his action, the transparency of the legal practice proper to a state church, a practice criticized by Rahner among others. A man of Rahner's theological and Christian stature can, in my opinion and that of many others, let pass the more personal reproaches which Cardinal Ratzinger, in his reply, raises against him.

Karl Rahner's testimony to the Christian and ecclesial character of my theology is all the more valuable to me in that it certainly in no way conceals the theological differences which exist between us, nor my own criticism of his theology. In this sense, I have always experienced him as a great theological teacher and friend. I would therefore like to dedicate this book to him as a token of this deep bond of friendship. I wish also to extend my gratitude to all those who have expressed their solidarity with me regarding this "case," whether publicly or in private.

Notes

1. Joseph Cardinal Höffner, "Pastoral der Kirchenfremden," opening report at the 1979 Autumn Plenary Session of the German Bishops' Conference in Fulda; published by the Sekretariat der Deutschen Bischofskonferenz, Kaiserstrasse 163, 5300 Bonn.
2. Ibid., pp. 65 ff.
3. Ibid., p. 43 n. 10.
4. Thus most recently in my contribution to the collective volume *Warum ich Christ bin,* ed. Walter Jens (Munich 1979), pp. 253–63.
5. K. Rahner, "Ich protestiere. Offener Brief an Kultusminister Hans Maier und Kardinal Joseph Ratzinger. Eine Wortmeldung zur Ablehnung von Johann Baptist Metz," in *Publik-Forum* no. 23 (16 November 1979): 15–19.
6. "Answer of the Archbishop of Munich and Freising, Joseph Cardinal Ratzinger, to the public criticisms of Professor Dr. Karl Rahner, S. J. regarding the nonappointment of Prof. Dr. Johann

Baptist Metz to the Chair of Fundamental Theology at the University of Munich'' originally appeared in *Ordinariats-Korrespondenz,* published by the Pressestelle des Erzbischöflichen Ordinariats München, no. 37 (13 December 1979): 2–4.

List of Sources

Messianic or Bourgeois Religion?
Address at the 1978 Catholic Congress (Katholikentag) in Freiburg, entitled "Glaube—Befähigung zur Zukunft?"; first published in *Ich will euch Zukunft und Hoffnung geben. 85. Deutscher Katholikentag vom 13. September bis 17. September 1978 in Freiburg* (Paderborn 1978), pp. 417–428; excerpts entitled "War nicht Jesus selbst in den Geruch des Verräters geraten?" in *Frankfurter Rundschau* no. 209 (21 September 1978) and "Eine Religion ohne messianische Zukunft," in *Süddeutsche Zeitung* no. 213 (16/17 September 1978); printed here in the version given in *Concilium* 15 (5/1979):308–315.

Christians and Jews after Auschwitz: Being a Meditation also on the End of Bourgeois Religion
Address at the 1978 Katholikentag in Freiburg during an event organized by the German Coordination Council for Christian-Jewish Collaboration, also at an ecumenical celebration for Reformation Day in Frankfurt in 1978; excerpts published under the title "Ökumene nach Auschwitz," in *Evangelische Kommentare* 12 (3/1979):137–140; published in its totality in E. Kogon and J. B. Metz, eds., *Gott nach Auschwitz. Dimensionen des Massenmordes am jüdischen Volk* (Freiburg 1979), pp. 122–144; also in *Freiburger Rundbrief* 30 (113–116/1978):7–13.

Bread of Survival: The Lord's Supper of Christians as
Anticipatory Sign of an Anthropological Revolution
Address at the 1979 German Evangelical Congress (Kirchentag) in
Nürnberg; first published in the official documentation volume of
the Kirchentag (Stuttgart-Berlin 1979), pp. 342–351; also in *Forum
Abendmahl*, ed. G. Kugler (Gütersloh 1979) (=*GTB aktuell* 346),
pp. 15–29.

Toward the Second Reformation:
The Future of Christianity in a Postbourgeois World
An address given at the 1979 Reformation Celebration in St. Mat-
thäus, Munich; first printed in three consecutive issues of the
Deutsches Allgemeines Sonntagsblatt nos. 2–4 (1980).

Christianity and Politics:
Beyond Bourgeois Religion
An address in 1980 in Erlangen to the Study Group "Kirchen und
SPD in Bayern"; hitherto unpublished.

Transforming a Dependent People:
Toward a Basic-Community Church
An address given at a discussion meeting during the 1980 "Katholikentag von unten" in Berlin; an abbreviated version entitled
"Den Panzer der bürgerlichen Religion durchbrechen" published
in the *Süddeutsche Zeitung* no. 130 (7/8 June 1980); printed here as
an extended version of " 'Wenn die Betreuten sich ändern . . .',
Von der befreienden Kraft einer Basiskirche," in *Publik-Forum* no.
13 (27 June 1980).

Paradigm for a Political Culture of Peace
The Laudatio in honor of Ernesto Cardenal at the ceremony award-
ing him the Peace Prize of the German book trade in the Pauls-
kirche, Frankfurt am Main on 12 October 1980; first published in
the *Börsenblatt für den Deutschen Buchhandel,* Frankfurt edition,
no. 86 (1980).

The Faith of the Reformers
A spontaneous talk given to students of the University of Münster
in 1968; transcript printed in *Publik* no. 13 (20 December 1968);

partially adapted version in J. B. Metz, *Reform und Gegenreformation heute. Zwei Thesen zur ökumenischen Situation der Kirchen* (Mainz-Munich, 1969); printed here in the slightly revised version of the *Publik* article.